Paddle Steamers

1837 to 1914

introduction and commentaries by

RICHARD CLAMMER

B.T. Batsford Ltd · *London*

for Carol

First published 1980
Text copyright © Richard Clammer

ISBN 0 7134 2331 5

Filmset in 'Monophoto' Apollo by
Servis Filmsetting Limited, Manchester
Printed in Great Britain by
Butler & Tanner Limited, Frome, Somerset
for the publishers B.T. Batsford Limited
4 Fitzhardinge Street, London W1H 0AH

The illustrations used as end papers are from an original plan in the Author's collection, entitled 'Longitudinal Section, P.S. *Britannia* or *Strathmore*, builders, Russell & Co, Port Glasgow.' These two ships were built in 1897 for John Williamson & Company, but only the *Strathmore* initially entered his fleet. The *Britannia* had been laid down as the *Kylemore* but was sold and renamed whilst still on the stocks, and went south to run on the Sussex coast. In 1908 she returned to the Clyde, reassumed her original name and survived until August 1940 when she was sunk whilst minesweeping in the Wash. The *Strathmore* remained on the Clyde until 1908 when she was sold to the Admiralty for service as a tender and re-named *Harlequin*. She had the distinction of being one of the last paddle steamers owned by the Royal Navy, and finally became a casualty in 1943

Contents

Acknowledgments

During the compilation of this book the author has received a great deal of generous assistance from a large number of different people, and would like to acknowledge his debt to the following firms, institutions and individuals: Her Majesty the Queen; Aberdeen University Library; Mr. J. Allendale; Mr. J. Annan; Miss G. Bidson, Birkenhead Public Library; Mr. P. Chaplin; Mr. R. Chapman; Rev. D. Ridley Chesterton, World Ship Society; Mr. C.E.N. Childs, Librarian of Brunel University; The Clyde River Steamer Club; Mr. B. Cox; Miss F. Dimond, Royal Archives, Windsor Castle; Mr. J. Edgington, National Railway Museum; Mr. B. Eglon-Shaw, Sutcliffe Gallery, Whitby; Mr. F.E. Gibson, Isles of Scilly; Mr. R.B. Grice; Mr. C.B. Harley; Mr. W.E.R. Hallgarth; Mr. P. Hayden; Mr. J. Hendy; Mr. R.W. Higginbottom, Société Jersiase; Mr. F.W. Hopps; The Keeper of Records for Scotland; Mr. J. Lingwood, Pacific Steam Navigation Co. Ltd; Mr. J. Lucking; Manchester Ship Canal Co; Mr. R. Mayne; The National Maritime Museum; National Library of Ireland; Osborne Studios (Falmouth) Ltd; Mr. G. Pattinson, Windermere Steamboat Museum; Mr. J. Renton; Scarborough Borough Council; Scarborough Public Library; 'Sea Breezes'; Mr. R. Shopland, Editor of 'Ships Monthly' and 'Waterways World'; Mr. P. Slater, Area Librarian, Gainsborough Public Library; Mr. M.K. Stammers, Keeper of Shipping, Merseyside County Museums; Mr. J.H. Syme, Scottish Record Office; Mr. E.C.B. Thornton; Mr. G.B. Vaughton; Mr. P. Vicary, Maritime Photo Library; Mrs. Pauline Watson; Miss R. Watson, Greater London Council Photographic Librarian; Mr. P. White.

In particular the author is greatly indebted to: Mrs. Pat Rooker, for typing the manuscript; Mr. Mike Tattershall for printing many of the photographs; and to Messrs. Eric Payne, Ken Saunders, George Thomas, George Osbon, Phil Thomas and Graham Langmuir who, in addition to checking various of the chapters, generously allowed free access to their splendid photographic collections and patiently answered innumerable questions.

Finally, a thank you to my wife Carol, without whose constant encouragement all the rest would have come to naught.

The Author would like to thank the following for permission to reproduce the photographs which appear in this book: Her Majesty Queen Elizabeth II – 71, 73, 74, 75; Mr. J. Allendale – 100; T. & R. Annan & Sons Ltd – 54; Birkenhead Public Library – 35; Brunel University Library – 51, 52, 53; Mr. R. Chapman – 17; Mr. W.E.R. Hallgarth – 14, 24; Mr. F. Hopps – 26, 89, 92, 93; Mr. F.E. Gibson – 82; Greater London Council Photographic Library – 29, 30, 31; Mr. R.B. Grice – 107; The Keeper of Records for Scotland – 9, 10, 15, 16, 48, 104, 110, 111, 113, 115, 116, 119, 121; Mr. G. Langmuir – 3, 23, 27, 32, 55, 56, 57, 77, 86, 88, 95, 112; Mr. J. Lucking – 81; Merseyside County Museums – 36; The National Maritime Museum, London – 6, 60, 61, 69, 84; The National Railway Museum, York, Crown Copyright – 79, 80, 85, 87, 90, 91; Osborne Studios (Falmouth) Ltd. – 68; Mr. E.D.G. Payne – 2, 11, 13, 18, 21, 25, 28, 33, 34, 40, 41, 43, 44, 45, 66, 72, 83, 96; The Port of Manchester – 1; The Pacific Steam Navigation Company Ltd. – 46, 47, 49, 50; Mr. K. Saunders – 19, 20, 22, 37, 38, 39, 42, 102, 105, 106, 122; Société Jersiase – 58; The Sutcliffe Gallery, Whitby – 12; Mr. M. Tattershall – 99; Mr. P. Thomas – 5, 8; Capt. G. Thomas – 103, 108, 109, 118, 120; Mr. P.A. Vicary's Maritime Photo Library – 4, 59, 62, 63, 64, 65, 67, 70; The remaining photographs, number 7, 76, 78, 94, 97, 98, 101, 114, 117 are from the author's collection.

3   Pictured here hard at work on the Clyde, near Erskine Ferry, is the iron tug *Clyde*, built in 1851 for the Trustees of the Clyde Navigation. She spent her life attending the Trust's steam dredgers and towing trains of mud punts to and from the discharging grounds. To help her in this specialised work she was fitted with a crane on the fo'c'sle and bridge-controlled engines. When she was broken up in 1912, her engines were removed and re-erected beside the river at Renfrew, where they may be seen to this day.

Introduction

The study of the British paddle steamer is, to a great many people, one of abiding interest and considerable historical importance. Over the last few years, as the number of these fascinating craft left in service has gradually dwindled, several carefully researched and authoritative books have appeared, recording the histories of particular types of steamer, areas of operation, and individual companies.

Although some of its chapters do I believe break new ground, this book does not attempt to add significantly to the historical research which has already taken place. Instead it seeks to fill a gap in the literature by providing, in one volume, a concise but complete visual guide to all the major types of paddle steamer which frequented our ports in the days before the First World War. The Victorian and Edwardian period has been chosen because it was then that the paddle steamer was enjoying its heyday both in terms of variety and number. The historical notes to each chapter outline the chief characteristics and stages of development of the vessels in question, and will hopefully tempt readers to delve further into the references detailed in the bibliography.

The photographs, which form the substance of this book, stand as historical documents in their own right. They span a period when photography was developing from its infancy in the calotype, albumen-on-glass and wet-plate processes of the 1840s and 50s, to the relative sophistication of the 1880s when the introduction of the box camera and the celluloid roll film made amateur photography a practical possibility. Their quality therefore varies considerably. I have attempted to maintain a balance between the use of professionally-exposed glass plates, whose quality and precision is often quite superb; the commercially'produced post cards which show the ships in their working environments; and the amateur 'snap shots' which, although lacking in technical quality, often convey a feeling of spontaneity which the more formal pictures lack. Many of the photographs are extremely rare, and only a few of them have appeared in book form before. Those that have are included for the sake of completeness where no alternative was available, or simply because I found them irresistible!

It is my hope that the resulting selection will be considered both as an informative and representative illustration of the chief types of Victorian and Edwardian paddle steamers, and as an historically valuable and aesthetically pleasing collection of photographs in its own right.

R.C. *Sheffield, December 1978*

Tugs

4   The Great Yarmouth tug *Express* of 1870, towing the local smacks *C.I.G.*, *Fashion*, and *John Macey* to sea. Note her clinker hull, and the fact that her wheel is located on the main deck and not on the bridge as in later tugs

It is perhaps significant that two of the earliest attempts in Great Britain to apply steam power to ships resulted in the construction of tugs. In 1736 Jonathan Hulls patented a design for a tow-boat which used a Newcomen engine, acting through a system of ropes and pulleys, to drive a rather bizarre set of stern wheels. This was followed during the late 1700s by William Symmington's experiments which culminated in the construction of the famous *Charlotte Dundas* tug, which ran her trials on the Forth & Clyde Canal in March 1802. The little vessel demonstrated her efficiency by towing two heavily-laden sloops for 20 miles against a headwind in six hours.

The shipping community was not slow to appreciate the potential of steam towage, and by 1814 the first custom-built tugs were appearing. During that year the *Industry* and the *Trusty* were built on the Clyde as luggage boats-cum-tugs, and in 1816 the Thames received its first tug in the form of the little *Majestic*. Development after that date was rapid, and by the time Victoria succeeded to the throne in 1837 there were several hundreds of paddle tugs in the British ports.

It is unnecessary to seek far for an explanation of the speedy ascent of the steam tug during the nineteenth century: Britain's maritime trade during that period was prodigious. The demands generated by the possession of a huge overseas Empire; the growth of the export trade following the Industrial Revolution; and the vast, domestic coastal trade caused by the lack of speedy, cheap road transport all combined to keep an enormous fleet of merchant ships in full employment. Although the number of steamships engaged in these trades grew quickly as the century progressed, a significant portion of the British merchant fleet throughout the period was composed of sailing vessels which were, of course, subject to interference by the vagaries of the weather.

Before the advent of the steam tug, ship owners had been forced to accept delays with stoical resignation. Now, however, their ships could cheat calms, enter difficult harbours under formerly dangerous conditions, or be towed to sea against a headwind, all for the price of a few tons of coal. The time saved in this manner significantly increased the efficiency and earning-power of their ships so it is not surprising that the paddle tugs became extremely popular.

The early tugs were tiny vessels — the *Industry* measured only 70 ft × 14 ft 7 in with a gross tonnage of 53, and was typical of her type. Most were of wooden, clinker-built construction and had beamy, saucer-shaped hulls with either clipper or spoon bows. Power was provided by a single side-lever engine driving paddles with simple, radial, fixed floats, and steering was frequently by tiller.

Wooden hulls remained popular for many years,

but were gradually superceded by composite, or later still, iron or steel hulls. During the 1830s the feathering paddle float was finally perfected, and wheels using this device were fitted to most tugs since they offered an increase in efficiency of over 10% in smooth water. Practical considerations dictated that most tugs were built with straight stems in preference to the clipper bows of earlier days and improvements in boiler design made it possible to install more powerful engines.

With increased sophistication, however, the outward appearance of the tugs altered very little, and a standard design soon emerged: that of a flush-decked vessel with a straight stem, counter stern, a single funnel placed abaft the large paddle boxes, and the steering position either between the boxes, or, in later ships, on a small bridge deck built above the engine house. A large sampson post for towing was usually fitted in the bows, whilst the after deck sported two towing bridges or 'strongbacks'. A typical tug would have a length of between 70 and 120 feet, and a tonnage within a similar range.

There were of course variations from this standard design to meet special requirements or an owner's whim. With the introduction of twin boilers in the 1850s many tugs appeared with twin funnels placed athwartships, although it later became the norm to route both boiler flues up a single smoke-stack. Some of the finest examples of twin stack tugs were those owned by the London firm of William Watkins, whose *Cambria*, *India*, *Uncle Sam* and others were well-known for their distinctive but antiquated appearance. Other variations included several double-ended tugs for working in very confined spaces, although few of these were built after the introduction of twin disconnecting engines, which allowed tugs so fitted to turn in their own length. On the Manchester Ship Canal a breed of paddlers developed with huge sponsons running practically from bow to stern, to facilitate pivoting against lock walls and knuckles of quays without inflicting damage on the hull. The Royal Navy and several merchant owners built large, powerful tugs with two funnels, one forward and one aft of the paddle boxes. The finest examples were the Naval *Advice* class (124 ft × 27 ft and 412 g.t.), the Liverpool Steam Tug Company's *Pathfinder* of 1876 (161 ft 4 in × 24 ft 8 in and 377 g.t.) and W. & T. Jolliffe's *Great Britain* (154 ft 1 in × 23 ft 7 in and 300 g.t.) whose dimensions made them considerably larger than the average paddle tug of the day.

More examples could be cited, but the fact remains that the vast majority of British paddle tugs bore a strong family resemblance. From the middle of the century onwards this was partly because many of them came from a small number of specialist builders. The most famous of these were the Tyneside trio of

J.P. Reynoldson & Company, J.T. Eltringham & Company and Hepple & Company, all of which had yards in South Shields.

Another feature common to most paddle tugs was the type of engine used. Practically every tug was fitted with 'grasshopper' or half side-lever engines. This is a little surprising since the grasshopper was, in reality, little more sophisticated than James Watt's original beam engines, the chief difference being that the overhead beam of Watt's design had been replaced by two beams, one on either side of the cylinder, placed low down on the engine bed plate and pivoted at their ends rather than in the centre. The design had been superceded by the mid-1800s by a variety of more efficient marine engines – Napier's 'Steeple', Penn's oscillating engine, and numerous others. The question therefore remains as to why the builders of paddle tugs stuck conservatively to such an obviously outmoded form of propulsion.

The answers seem to be fourfold: Firstly, the grasshopper was a simple engine which was easy and cheap to make and install, and which could survive for long periods with only a minimum of skilled maintenance. Secondly, the presence of the two heavy side-levers at the base of the engine meant that the centre of gravity was kept low in the hull – an important factor in tugs, which were constantly exposed to the risk of capsizing if a tow was badly handled. Thirdly, the engines had an extremely long stroke, which made them well-suited to towing work, and lastly, the single-cylinder design meant that there was in practice no 'dead spot' on the crank shaft, which could be turned again from any position of rest, and so the engine could always be relied upon to react quickly to engine orders.

Needless to say, these advantages were offset by a number of disadvantages. Amongst these was the fact that when the engine was started from rest, it was impossible to predict which way the crankshaft would turn. Manipulating such wilful machinery was something of an art and required experienced and skilful engineers. The second disadvantage was arguably the greater since it contributed to the eventual decline of the tugs. This, quite simply, was the fact that the grasshopper engine used vast quantities of coal. Whilst this was not too serious in the early days, rising coal prices and the availability of economical screw tugs towards the end of the century gradually drove the paddle tug to extinction.

As tow boats paddle vessels had certain inherent advantages. Their immense breadth across the paddle boxes made them very stable, and their large clear decks were ideal for rope handling. The paddle wheels gave them enormous braking power, and as already mentioned, disconnecting engines enabled them to turn in their own length. These last two features made them particularly suitable for use in confined, crowded harbours, and long, winding river approaches, and it was in those settings that they survived longest.

Not all paddle tugs were limited to harbour work. From the large esturial ports powerful tugs such as the Watkins vessels, already referred to, went out to sea for several days at a time seeking homeward-bound sailing ships, with whom they would attempt to strike a bargain for the tow into port.

Less competitive than 'seeking', but far more dangerous, was the salvage work that many tugs undertook. In the age of sail, dismastings, wrecks and other mishaps were commonplace and there were large salvage awards to be had by any tug with a skilful and strong-nerved skipper. In many ports owners found it worthwhile to keep a tug on standby with steam up, ready to put to sea if the need arose. At the Dorset port of Weymouth, for example, the diminutive *Commodore* tug was known to carry out as many as three salvage jobs in one night, and to earn as much as £1,500 for a single service. This is all the more surprising when one realises that the little ship was only 93 ft long, with engines of a mere 60 H.P.

By the nature of their work, salvage tugs were called upon to operate in appalling weather conditions, and soon proved themselves to be more efficient than many of the contemporary sailing lifeboats. At several ports the RNLI recognised this and entered into formal contracts with the local tug companies to tow the lifeboats to the scene of disasters.

The paddle tug reigned supreme until the 1880s, by which time screw tugs were beginning to outclass the older paddlers, many of which found it difficult to pay their way. In the fishing ports, paddle tugs had been used regularly for towing fishing smacks to sea, and during calms it was not unknown for the fishermen to shoot their nets whilst still under tow. Finding that it was possible to trawl successfully in this manner, it was but a short step to equipping the paddlers themselves for trawling. The first experiments seem to have been carried out at North Shields in 1877, when the tug *Messenger* was equipped very successfully with a beam trawl. Within a few years, large numbers of redundant paddle tugs were being converted by the simple addition of trawling gear and a sampson post abaft the funnel for hauling the nets.

Paddle trawlers worked from many British ports, but the greatest concentration was to be found in the traditional East Coast fishing ports. Bridlington, Scarborough, Shields, Whitby and others all boasted large fleets. The paddlers were limited to inshore fishing since they could not carry ice and were therefore unable to stay at sea for more than a day or two before landing their catches, and many of them were so old that they literally fell to pieces under the strain of fishing. Another factor which militated against the paddle trawlers was the invention of the otter trawl. After some experimentation it was realised that the paddle wheels and boxes effectively prevented the paddlers from using the new method and so, once custom-built screw trawlers began to appear, it did not take long for the paddlers to fall from favour. It seems that the loss of the last Scarborough paddle trawler, the *Constance*, off Hartlepool in 1910, marked the end of an era. The last paddlers to be used for fishing were probably the little fleet of oyster dredgers built towards the end of the nineteenth century to work the oyster beds of the rivers Blackwater, Irwell and Colne in Essex. The story of these craft is somewhat clouded, but it seems that the last of them survived into the 1950s, and was occasionally used for towing work.

With the growth of the Victorian fashion for seaside holidays, other tug owners found that they could boost their income by running summer excursion sailings. Many tugs spent the winter employed in towage, and worked the holiday trade during the summer months. This was so lucrative that some companies found it worth their while to build dual-purpose vessels, a fine example of which was the Weymouth tug *Queen* of 1883, which had two fine saloons upholstered in 'best Utrecht velvet'. Access to the passenger accommodation was by way of specially designed mahogany companion ways, which could be dismantled and sealed against heavy seas should the tug be required for salvage work.

In all its different guises, the paddle tug remained popular until well into the 1890s. Thereafter, the number of new tugs ordered began to fall rapidly, and although some were built for specialised jobs, building had virtually ceased by 1914 leaving the screw tug to reign supreme. Natural wastage thinned the paddlers' ranks over the years, but, fortunately for posterity, the tugs' hardy construction and cheap-to-maintain engines made them an economic proposition in the North Eastern coal ports until quite recently. The last Edwardian paddle tug, the *Reliant* (ex *Old Trafford*), built in 1907 for the Manchester Ship Canal Company and transferred to Seaham Harbour in 1950, was not withdrawn until 1969. She was then purchased by the National Maritime Museum, and is now preserved as the centre piece of the Neptune Hall at Greenwich.

6 ABOVE William Watkins' famous *Anglia* of 1866, was one of the most noteworthy tugs ever built. Designed for long-distance open-sea towing, she had 700 H.P. engines and three boilers, the latter fact accounting for her unique funnel layout which can be seen clearly in this photograph. Known habitually as 'Three-fingered Jack', she undertook many long and difficult tows, the most celebrated of which involved bringing Cleopatra's Needle from Vigo on the final stage of its ill-starred voyage from Egypt in 1877, during the earlier stages of which it had broken away from its original tug and spent several days adrift in a gale in the Bay of Biscay

5 Built by J. Readhead of South Shields in 1874, the *Ulysses* was a typical example of a tug with twin funnels placed athwartships. She spent her early life on the Thames, but returned to the North East in 1895, under the ownership of the Lawson Batey Steam Tug Company of Newcastle

7 BELOW This view of the Weymouth tug *Albert Victor* putting to sea in the teeth of an easterly gale to assist a ship in distress off Portland, gives some idea of the appalling weather conditions in which many small salvage tugs were expected to work

8   Seen here at Eastham Locks on the Manchester Ship
Canal, the steel tug *Acton Grange* was in most respects
typical of the latter-day paddle tugs build by the
Tyneside yard of J. T. Eltringham. Her sponsons,
however, were extended further fore and aft than was
normal in harbour tugs in order to give increased
protection to her hull whilst working in the canal locks.
Acton Grange was used chiefly as a stern tug and was
therefore fitted with massive towing bits on her
foredeck, and these can be seen clearly in the
photograph. She was broken up in 1951, but her sister
ship *Old Trafford* survived, and is now preserved as the
Reliant in the National Maritime Museum

9 Lying in the fitting-out basin of John Brown's yard on Clydebank shortly before her delivery to the Admiralty in April 1902, the *Energetic* makes an imposing sight. She was one of a class of tugs built for the Navy around the turn of the century, and with a gross tonnage of 412 tons, was considerably larger than the average merchant tug of the period. The class was rendered distinctive by its funnel layout – one forward and one aft of the engines – and by the fact that oscillating engines were fitted in preference to the more usual side-lever type

10 This rare view of the crew's fo'c'sle of the *Energetic* contrasts with some of the plush excursion steamer saloons pictured later in this book. Although roomier than most, the layout of this fo'c'sle, with its oil lamp, coal stove and wooden lockers, is typical of those found in most coastal ships of the period. Note the twin anchor cables passing from the deck to the cable locker below – the noise and filth caused by the rapid passage of the rusty chain when the tug dropped anchor can have contributed little to the homeliness of this spartan compartment!

11 RIGHT A typical paddle trawler of the 1890s, the *Triumph* of Scarborough, here seen leaving her home port for the fishing grounds. She is carrying an 'otter-trawl' in preference to the old fashioned 'beam-trawl' used by earlier paddlers and smacks. The trawl-doors or 'otter boards', used to keep the mouth of the net open, can be seen; one on the sponson, and one suspended from the bulwark at the stern. This is most unusual as it was normally regarded as impractical for paddlers to use the otter trawl, whose invention effectively put an end to the paddle trawler era

12 RIGHT This tranquil scene captured by the famous Whitby photographer Frank Meadow Sutcliffe, shows the Glasgow tug *Flying Spray* high and dry on the harbour mud during her sojourn as an East Coast trawler, c.1897. She is fitted with the usual derrick for handling the nets and the end of her heavy trawl beam is visible, projecting from behind her port quarter

13   This beautiful study was taken on 16 August 1907, shortly after the Jarrow tug *Saxon Prince* (M. Dickenson, master) had gone ashore at Saltcar Rocks on the Yorkshire Coast whilst on passage from Jarrow to Port Mulgrave with a lighter in tow. The crowd of onlookers probably did not realise that they were witnessing the last hours of the old ship, which went to pieces during the next day, 17 August. An 89 ton wooden clinker-built vessel of the old style, the *Saxon Prince* was built in 1884 for W. H. Storey of South Shields and sold to George Todd of Jarrow sometime between 1900 and 1906

14 The Grimsby tug *Humber* in use as a summer excursion steamer, landing passengers at Spurn Head, *c.*1900. Judging by the proximity of her stern to the ferry boat and landing stage, she must be at anchor with only a few inches of water under her keel

15 RIGHT Another large Admiralty tug, the *Rambler* is seen here fitting out at John Brown's yard in January 1909. Her dimensions were similar to those of the *Energetic*, but her profile was more conventional. She was finally broken up in 1955, after a long and active career

16 BELOW The engines of the *Rambler*. The ships of her class differed radically from most merchant tugs in having two sets of compound diagonal engines in place of the usual side-lever type

River & Lake Steamers

17 The little *Reindeer* is thought to have maintained a connecting service between the Great Western Railway station at Kingsbridge and the Devon village of Salcombe, where this picture was taken. The heavily built *Reindeer* was the predecessor to the more shapely *Ilton Castle* and *Kenwith Castle* which subsequently operated these sailings. It was not until 1927, long after the demise of the *Reindeer*, that the G.W.R. took over control of the river steamers, which before that date were all privately owned. The tops'l schooner in the background is the *Edward* of Guernsey

For many years prior to the advent of the steamboat, the major rivers and estuaries of Britain had been used as important water-highways which, although subject to periods of flood and drought, were often considerably more efficient than the badly kept and frequently impassable roads of the day. Heavy goods were more easily transported by water than by packhorse or carrier's waggon, and the savings in time and cost were sometimes so great that it was considered worthwhile to widen, deepen or canalise some rivers in order to move their heads of navigation further inland.

In response to the navigational peculiarities and trade requirements of individual waterways, as well as to local boat building traditions and skills, many distinctive fleets of sail-traders came into being. The sloops and keels of Yorkshire, the Severn Trows, the Mersey Flats and the Thames Spritsail barges were but a few of these highly localised craft, whose designs had evolved slowly over the years. Although they were relatively efficient, these old craft were bound by the limitations of all sailing vessels. Adverse winds or strong river flows could delay them for days, and the barges were frequently sculled or towed by hand to their destinations.

The earliest steamboats had shown their ability to overcome these problems by towing such barges along rivers and canals, and once their efficiency was confirmed it was not long before river steamers became established as passenger and cargo carriers in their own right. The inefficient boilers and small engines of the early days of steam were not such a crippling disadvantage on rivers as they might have been at sea, for the ships they powered were smaller, unhampered by tows, and never far from coal supplies and repair yards. It is hardly surprising therefore that the use of steam ships on British rivers burgeoned rapidly during the first half of the nineteenth century.

1814 seems to be a significant date on the British rivers, for in that year the *Marjory* came into service as the first Thames steamboat, the *Caledonia* made the first trip from Gainsborough to Hull by way of the Trent and Humber, the aptly named *Tay* appeared on the river of that name, the *Industry* was built on the Clyde, and the *Tyne Steamboat* entered service on the Tyne. Thereafter the river fleets grew quickly and by the beginning of the period with which we are concerned, numbered several hundred vessels.

A word is perhaps necessary on the meaning of the term 'river steamer'. It is true that many river steamers were in fact tugs pressed into service as passenger craft, whilst on some rivers, especially the large estuaries like the Clyde and Thames, the vessels employed were in reality sea-going passenger ships. Likewise, many ferry steamers doubled as river excursion boats. But for the purpose of this chapter,

river steamers can be defined as those vessels which were designed primarily to operate in sheltered river waters, and to maintain communications between places along the banks of those rivers, using the river itself as a linear routeway. Although some overlap must inevitably exist, ferries (ie those vessels designed to carry land routeways across water barriers) and esturial excursion steamers are dealt with elsewhere in the book.

It is also interesting to note how the design of British river steamers developed. The pioneer vessels of the 1830s and 40s had no regional characteristics – indeed they were frequently nomadic – but as regular services became established, local designs emerged in exactly the same way as they had done with the older sailing barges. In some cases this change was simply due to the tastes or foibles of an owner or a local shipyard (for in most cases the ships were built locally) and an initial characteristic was often perpetuated in later ships due to innate conservatism. More positively, the ships were designed with particular trades in mind, and often with the benefit of long experience, so designs evolved accordingly.

On the beautiful rias of the Salcombe River and the River Dart in South Devon, the local design crystallised after about 1880. The Dart steamers (latterly owned by the River Dart Steamboat Company) operated between Dartmouth and Totnes, picking up local passengers, goods and farm produce en route, whilst the Salcombe vessels were designed to connect Salcombe with the rail head at Kingsbridge, further up the river. The natural beauties of the area encouraged the growth of a tourist trade which continued to expand up until the First World War; and combined with the sheltered conditions experienced on these rivers, led to the development of a series of dainty little steamers with broad beams, well-decks fore and aft, and a single funnel abaft the paddle boxes. They came from local yards like Harvey & Company of Hayle, Philip & Son of Dartmouth or Cox & Son of Falmouth. Another feature common to both fleets was the nomenclature of the steamers, all of which were named after castles. Two of the ex-River Dart boats are still afloat – the *Compton Castle* of 1914 at Looe, and the *Kingswear Castle* of 1924 at Rochester – and presently undergoing restoration. Although neither was built within our period, their appearance is practically identical to their predecessors' and the *Kingswear Castle* is even fitted with engines built in 1904 for a previous ship of the same name.

At the other end of the river steamer scale came the vessels built for service on the Rivers Trent, Ouse and Humber. All three rivers are liable to floods and the Trent has the added hazard of a tidal bore or aegre which can be dangerous to small vessels. Below the confluence of the Trent and Ouse, at Trent Falls, the shallow Humber flows in a wide estuary beset by savage tidal flows and constantly shifting mud banks, and is liable to weather conditions more frequently associated with the open sea. It follows therefore that the ships built to operate in this area were larger, stronger ships, built on sea-going lines.

The two major companies in the area were the Hull & Goole Steam Packet Company and the Gainsborough United Steam Packet Company, which maintained regular services between Gainsborough, Goole, Hull and Grimsby, calling en route at small riverside villages like Barton, Ferriby and Burton Stather to collect local people, their goods and livestock. The scene on the deck of the Gainsborough 'Market Boat' on a choppy day must have been animated indeed!

Most other British river steamers fell somewhere between these extremes of design. All of the major rivers – the Thames, Tees, Tyne, Forth, Tay, Mersey and Clyde – boasted fleets, as did many of the smaller rivers. Before the First World War it was possible, for example, to sail from Poole up the Frome to Wareham by the *P.S. Wareham Queen*, from Deganwy to Trefriw up the Conway by one of the St. George Steam Packet Company's pretty little ships, or to travel by paddle steamer on the Tamar or Shannon. Since the demise of the steamers, many of these smaller rivers have become silted and overgrown to such an extent that it is difficult to imagine how a fair-sized vessel ever made the passage.

Predictably for the river which runs through our largest city, the Thames supported a vast fleet of river steamers, which carried out the functions now fulfilled by buses and underground railways. During the 1830s and 40s four major companies were in competition on the river, employing well over 40 steamers to transport passengers between the numerous piers along both banks of the Thames from Woolwich up to Kew, Richmond and Lambeth. By 1871 the four companies – the Woolwich S.P. Company, the Iron Steamboat Company, the Watermans S.P. Company, and the Citizen Steam Boat company – had amalgamated, and by 1876 control had passed to the London Steamboat Company whose vast fleet numbered a total of 70 vessels. This company suffered a severe blow in 1878 when their down-river excursion steamer *Princess Alice* was in collision with a collier whilst homeward bound one evening on the Thames. *Princess Alice* broke in two and sank quickly with an immense loss of life, and the incident went down in history as the worst-ever excursion steamer disaster. The resulting publicity caused public enthusiasm for river excursions to fall away rapidly, and the company never recovered, its vessels being sold by auction in 1884.

The new owners were the River Thames Steamboat Company, but they too were soon in trouble. Competition from the trams, omnibuses and railways caused a fall in passenger figures, and in 1890 the company sold out to the Victoria Steamboat Association. When the latter company withdrew in 1902, the London County Council applied for powers to run a river fleet in the belief that the service was needed and would ease traffic congestion in the capital. The service was inaugurated on 17 June, 1905 by the Prince of Wales in the paddler *King Alfred*, but the 'penny steamers', like their predecessors, were doomed to failure and the fleet of 30 new steamers was withdrawn and sold in October 1909. It is curious indeed that Britain's largest and busiest river seemed unable to support a steamer service!

In addition to the rivers, some interesting services operated on various British lakes and canals. It is recorded that some of the early Humber steamers ventured into the canal system at Keadby lock on the Trent and sailed to Thorne to connect with the London stagecoach, but this practice is thought to have died out before the beginning of the Victorian era.

In Scotland, a succession of paddle steamers worked on the Caledonian Canal between Inverness and Banavie. In the early days the ships were owned by David Hutcheson and others, but after about 1879 ownership passed to David MacBrayne, whose fleet continued the service until its demise in 1939. The four most famous names associated with the canal, together with their dates of service on the waterway, were the *Gondolier* (1866–1939), *Glengarry* (1845–1927), *Gairlochy* (1894–1919), and *Lochness* (1885–1912). The former ship was built especially for the service, but the other three were transferred from elsewhere and altered to suit. All the ships were fair-sized, good-looking saloon steamers of similar appearance to their sea-going fleet mates, but all were fitted with unconventional, convex, canoe-shaped bows to enable them to work through the canal locks without damage. A mail service was operated between Fort Augustus and Inverness, and the through route, passing through Loch Ness, was extremely popular with excursion passengers.

In Ireland an extensive network of services existed on the loughs and rivers before the First War. In the South, Lough Corrib, Lough Derg and the Shannon all boasted paddlers, whilst in the North, Lough Erne received its first paddle steamer, the *Countess of Erne*, in December 1842, and Lough Gill followed suit a year later with the *Lady Of The Lake*.

Loch Lomond, in Scotland, has supported passenger paddle steamers since 1817. The pioneer vessel, David Napier's 57 ton, wooden *Marion*, which lasted on the Loch until 1832, was soon imitated by several other small steamers. By the time that the ownership of the Loch Lomond fleet passed into railway hands in 1888, a 'standard' design had emerged which owed a great deal to the profiles of the contemporary Clyde steamers.

In view of the persistence of paddle propulsion on Loch Lomond (as indeed on the European Lakes where large fleets exist to this day) it is interesting to speculate as to why paddle steamers fell from fashion so quickly on other British inland waters. From the earliest days Lochs Awe, Eck and Katrine were served by screw vessels, and the paddlers did not last very long in Ireland. England, admittedly, has few lakes large enough to support steamer services, but even the largest of them, Lake Windermere, rejected paddles in favour of the screw propellor as early as the 1870s.

The first Windermere paddle steamer, the *Lady Of The Lake*, was built in 1845 by R. Ashburner of Newby Bridge and measured 80 ft × 11 ft 5 in × 6 ft 4 in. Although a great success, she met with considerable resentment from some of the local populace, who regarded the advent of the vulgar steamboat as something to be resisted. In his 'Itinerary Poems of 1833', the Lake poet Wordsworth had grudgingly accepted the coming of the steamboat as an inevitable blot upon the loveliness of nature, and combined with the later conservative attitudes of the local people to the *Lady*, gave *Punch* magazine a fine opening for a little gentle satire, in the form of the following poem, lampooning a style which is not too hard to recognise!:

What Incubus, my goodness! have we here,
Lumb'ring the bosom of our lovely lake?
A steamboat, as I live! – Without mistake!
Puffing and splashing over Windermere!
What inharmonious shouts assail mine ear,
Shocking poor Echo that perforce replies –
'Ease her, and stop her'. Frightful, horrid cries
Mingling with the frequent pop of ginger beer.

Hence ye profane! To Greenwich or Blackwall,
From London Bridge – go! Steam it if you will
Ye Cockneys! And of whitebait eat your fill
But this is not the place for you at all!
I almost think that, if I had my will
I'd sink your vessel with a cannonball.

As it happened, steamer services were a great success on the lake, and it became a fashionable local pastime to keep a steam launch for pleasure. One or two of these little private steamers were paddle driven. The *Lady of The Lake*'s owners introduced a second ship, the *Lord of the Isles*, in 1846, and in 1849 the Windermere Iron Steamboat Company came into opposition with the *Firefly* and *Dragonfly*. The two companies amalgamated in 1858, and the last Windermere paddler, the *Rothay*, was launched in 1866, after which date all subsequent steamers were screw driven. The wreck of a paddle steamer, thought to be the *Rothay*, has recently been located on the bed of the lake, and there is a possibility that she may be raised.

The popularity of river and lake steamer services grew throughout the Victorian and Edwardian periods. Competition from the railways and improved roads with steam and later motor haulage, caused a steady decline in trade on those services, like the Trent market boats, which relied chiefly on the carriage of goods and livestock. Excursion sailings on the more attractive stretches of water increased in popularity and went far to offset the decline in other areas. Many services which had started life with utilitarian purposes, were gradually transformed into summer-only pleasure sailings. In this guise some, like the River Dart services, survived well into the present century when they too collapsed – victims of changing tastes and lack of patronage.

18 Heavily laden with excursionists, the Dartmouth Steam Packet Company's *Berry Castle* is pictured here approaching Dartmouth Quay after sailing downstream from Totnes. Built in 1880, her design was so successful that all subsequent Dart and Salcombe steamers were broadly similar in appearance and internal layout. *Berry Castle* and the next vessel built for the service were fitted with 2-cylinder oscillating engines, but from 1894 onwards all new ships received compound diagonal machinery

19 The Salcombe River steamer *Ilton Castle* landing
passengers during a summer excursion, *c*.1907.
Maintaining one's dignity whilst jumping or wading
ashore from an open boat in the voluminous clothes of
the day must have posed a considerable problem for
the average Edwardian lady!

20 This view of Deganwy, on the River Conway in North Wales, shows two of the St. George Steamship Company's little paddle steamers which maintained a passenger service between Deganwy, Conway and Trefriw at the head of navigation. The *Prince George* of 1891 is lying alongside the pier whilst the younger *King George* of 1907 is hurrying upstream towards Conway on the opposite bank. Judging by the way in which the passengers on both ships are huddled beneath the deck-awnings, the North Wales weather was equally unpredictable then. Steamer services on the river began in about 1847 with the iron paddler *St George*, and ceased in 1940 when the *King George* was finally withdrawn

21 RIGHT Weaving her way down the River Yealm towards Plymouth is the *Empress*, built in 1880 for the Devon and Cornwall Tamar Steam Packet Company. In 1891 her owners were bought out by William Gilbert of Saltash who, having disposed of all opposition, formed the famous Saltash, Three Towns and District Steamboat Company which continued to run pleasure sailings round Plymouth Sound, to the Yealm, and up the Tamar until its last steamers, the *Alexandra* and *Prince Edward*, were broken up in 1928

22 BELOW Built in 1898 for the Dumbarton and Balloch Joint Committee's Loch Lomond services, the *Princess May* is seen here at Balloch Pier at the southern end of the lake. Together with her sister *Prince George* she was typical of the large, spacious, 'classic' Loch Lomond steamers of the period, except that they were the first to have their after saloons carried out to the full width of the hull. *Princess May* had a long life, and was finally broken up on the loch side in 1953

THE LOCKS, FORT AUGUSTUS. 14932. J.V.

23 LEFT MacBraynes' famous *Gondolier* of 1866, locking down through the Fort Augustus locks on the Caledonian Canal around the turn of the century. After spending her whole working life on the canal this much-loved ship was withdrawn in 1939 and her hull was sunk during the Second War as a blockship at Scapa Flow. In common with many steamers of her period, *Gondolier* was fitted with oscillating engines and, as this picture clearly shows, had a narrow deck saloon aft with alleyways round the outside. In later steamers it was normal to carry the deck saloons out to the full width of the hull

24 ABOVE The landing stage at Burton Stather, with the Gainsborough United Steam Packet Company's steamer *Atalanta* of 1851 berthed alongside. Together with her fleet-mates *Scarborough* and *Isle of Axeholme* she maintained a regular cargo and passenger service between Gainsborough and Hull, calling at a number of villages en route, as well as sailing to and from Grimsby and offering seasonal river and sea excursions

25 The crew of the Gainsborough steamer *Scarborough*, c.1900. *Scarborough* was the pride of the Trent fleet, but spent much of her time running summer excursions from the seaside resort whose name she bore. During the holiday season the steamer carried a band of three musicians in addition to her normal deck and engine room staff. She made her final sailing from Scarborough on 4 September 1914

26 RIGHT Taken in 1895, this photograph shows the *Isle of Axeholme* at the Gainsborough Steam Packet Wharf on the River Trent. Moored on the inside berth is the *Atalanta*, minus her funnel and presumably undergoing a winter refit. The picture gives a good idea of the extent and nature of the riverside industry of the day

27 Lambeth Pier with one of the Citizen Steamboat Company's up-river Thames steamers alongside. The company was formed in 1846 and owned 18 iron steamers which were identified alphabetically as *Citizen A-S* (omitting *I*). Each steamer wore its name and letter plus the arms of the City of London on the outboard surface of each paddle box, and on the inboard surfaces a scroll (one is clearly visible in this photograph) bearing the name of one of the City Guilds. Thus the London River was graced by such bizarrely-named vessels as the *Spectacle-Maker*, the *Leather-Seller* and the *Fishmonger*! This particular photograph is something of a mystery since the vessel is un-lettered and therefore unidentified. She is double-ended, and the bow rudder in its aperture together with the wheel on the deck above can be seen

28 RIGHT The *Fuchsia* (ex *Citizen F*) was built at Battersea in 1872, and with an overall length of 127 ft 6 in and a tonnage of 77 tons was typical of the upper Thames steamers of the 1870s and 80s. Originally owned by the Citizen S.B. Company, she subsequently changed hands three times during the sales and amalgamations outlined in the introduction. This picture was taken at Putney Pier between 1885 and 1891

29 RIGHT One of the London County Council's ill-fated river steamers, the *Colechurch* was built by Napier & Miller & Company, of Glasgow at a cost of £6,000, sold only four years later on 20 July 1907 for a mere £500, and saw further use on Lake Lugano. All the L.C.C. boats had roughly the same dimensions –
130 ft × 18 ft × 6 ft 8 in – and were fitted with compound diagonal engines which gave them a speed of 10 knots. 530 passengers could be carried, and fares were based on penny stages. The latter feature earned the boats the nickname of the 'penny steamers'

30 LEFT The saloon of the *Olaf*, another of the L.C.C. fleet. The boats operated a regular service at 15-minute intervals from 7.00 a.m. to 6.30 p.m. all the year round, and little saloons such as this, however bare and functional they may appear to the modern eye, provided welcome warmth and shelter for passengers during the winter months

31 BELOW, LEFT The Prince of Wales, later King George V, landing from the *King Alfred* after inaugurating the L.C.C.'s 'penny steamer' service on 17 June 1905. This ambitious attempt to revive London's steamer services on a grand scale served 23 piers between Greenwich and Hammersmith, but was extremely short-lived. Such a huge loss was made that the service was abandoned in October 1909, and the fleet of 30 specially-built steamers was sold

32 BELOW These two elegant little paddle launches have not been positively identified, but are believed to be the *Thames* (*right*) and the *Isis* (*left*) which operated a regular summer service between Folly Bridge, Oxford (where this photograph was taken) and Kingston. The placards on the pier advertise short trips to Iffley every evening and excursions to Nuneham on Tuesdays and Thursdays. The boats' owners were the Thames and Isis Steam Packet Company, formed in 1878, who were the predecessors to the famous fleet of screw steamers owned by Salter Bros. In addition to the two paddlers, the company is thought to have owned at least one screw launch, and to have ceased operating after the 1882 season

THE ISIS, FROM FOLLY BRIDGE, OXFORD. 3554 GWW

33 The Great Eastern Railway's double-ended steamer *Essex*, built in 1896 for the company's services between Ipswich, Harwich and Felixstowe on the Rivers Orwell and Stour, is seen here approaching Felixstowe Old Pier on one of her summer excursion sailings. Her near-sister *Suffolk* and the similar but single-funnelled *Norfolk* continued to operate on the river until 1931, but *Essex* left the fleet in 1913, and after passing through various hands, was sold abroad in October 1918

34 The 'Ha'penny Ferry' pontoon at North Shields was typical of the type of floating jetties which many ferries utilised in an attempt to offer a regular service at all states of the tide. Pulling away from the pontoon is the *Collingwood*, which maintained the North–South Shields service for many years. Note how her broad fo'c'sle has been left uncluttered, whilst the upper deck aft has been raised to bulwark level to allow space for a small saloon beneath

Designed with the simple, utilitarian aim of carrying lines of land communication across natural water barriers, the workaday ferries of Victorian and Edwardian Britain were the most unsung of paddle steamers. Required to maintain reliable, regular services in all weather conditions, all the year round, they usually lacked the fine lines and ornate decoration of their coastal and cross-channel cousins and were built to severely functional designs. Furthermore, many of the ferry routes were located in heavily urbanised areas and tended to attract the attentions of none but their regular, essential users, with the consequences that in comparison with other types of paddle steamer they were rather scantily documented by contemporary photographers.

For the sake of convenience, ferries may be divided into three main categories. The smallest type, whose appearance differed radically from place to place, ran on the shorter routes across the narrower rivers and on the upper reaches of our major estuaries. Typical examples would be the routes from Dartmouth to Kingswear across the Dart, from Cardiff to Penarth across the Ely, the various Tyne and Tees ferries, the Tilbury and Woolwich crossings of the Thames, and the multiplicity of routes from Liverpool across the Mersey.

Esturial ferries made up the second group, and as might be expected of vessels operating in wider, more exposed waters, tended to be larger and more weatherly in design than their up-river counterparts, although bearing a strong family resemblance to them. Both types were characterised by shallow draft hulls which were extremely beamy in relation to their length, by long, heavy, protective sponsons, and in many cases by at least one easily accessible, uncluttered deck. The Hull to New Holland ferry across the Humber, the Queensferry passage of the Forth, and the routes across the Tay were all good examples.

The third category was composed of those vessels whose routes took them into the open sea. The steamers which ran from Lymington, Southampton, Portsmouth and Southsea to the Isle of Wight fell into this grouping, and closely resembled the excursion steamers of their day. The development of excursion steamer design is dealt with elsewhere in this book, so at this point it is sufficient to say that during our period both types developed along almost identical lines, from the early vessels with open maindecks fore and aft, to the familiar saloon vessels with deck saloons aft and large open foredecks, which were to be seen in the Solent right up until the 1950s.

All ferries spent the bulk of their time manoeuvring alongside piers or threading their way across the flow of traffic and tide in rivers and narrow channels, and paddle propulsion was ideally suited to this type of employment. The heavy sponsons afforded protection to the hull whilst berthing, and the paddles themselves made the ships easy to stop or put astern. Disconnecting engines were an innovation adopted by many ferries, which were thus rendered even more manoeuvrable than previously, and the extra beam caused by the paddle boxes and sponsons greatly increased their carrying capacity and stability. To assist working in extremely confined channels, where swinging the vessel at the end of each sailing was clearly impractical or inconvenient, many ferries were double-ended, and were fitted with rudders at both bow and stern.

Until the introduction of twin-screw propulsion, no other vessels could compete with the paddler on ferry routes, and even when the screw did become established, the paddlers hung on for many years on some services, their relatively shallow draft often being the deciding factor. The last regular steam paddle ferry, the *Lincoln Castle*, was not withdrawn from the Hull–New Holland route until 1978, and even now a diesel paddle vessel, the *Farringford*, is used on that shallow-water service.

In the early days a wide variety of paddlers was employed on ferry sailings. The first Mersey ferry, for example, was the second-hand Clyde ship *Elizabeth*, and several of her successors on the Mersey service also doubled as tugs. Similar situations existed on other rivers, where steam quickly replaced sail on most of the old-established routes, and made crossings so much faster and more reliable that a number of new routes were inaugurated.

As these developments were taking place, purpose-built ferries began to appear and regional characteristics emerged in response to the requirements of individual routes. Speed of discharge and loading were of the essence, so many vessels were either fitted with large folding gangways or ramps, which could be lowered quickly when berthing to allow vehicles and foot passengers to clear the ship rapidly, or with large doors in the bulwarks which, when opened, would allow mechanical ramps to be lowered from the jetty or pontoon. In order to assist their masters in laying them gently and swiftly alongside at frequent intervals, many ferries were fitted either with conning positions on the paddle boxes or with exceptionally broad bridges, the wings of which often extended to the full beam of the ferry, thus allowing the captain a clear view of the whole length of his ship. Other variations included stern doors, as fitted to the Isle of Wight steamer *Victoria* of 1860, and twin-hulled, catamaran-form vessels such as some of the early Tay ferries. In addition there were, of course, the multitude of smaller design differences which were the natural result of the preferences of individual owners and builders.

It is also interesting to note how the nature of many

ferry routes changed through time. Once the efficiency of steam was established there was frequently heated competition between alternative routes across the same rivers. On the Humber, for example, it used to be possible to cross between Hull and New Holland, Ferriby Sluice, Grimsby or Barton, whilst on the Mersey, routes existed between Liverpool and eleven destinations on the opposite bank. Urban rivers like the Tyne and Tees were capable of supporting several short routes, and even the relatively rural West-Country rivers like the Fal and the Tamar boasted a respectable fleet of steamers.

With the coming of the railways, however, some rationalisation took place, especially amongst the esturial ferry routes. Before the building of major structures like the Forth and Tay railway bridges, Britain's larger estuaries provided an irritating stumbling-block to rapid, efficient rail travel on many routes, and the railway companies sought to minimise delays by buying out existing ferry companies or inaugurating their own routes. In order to attract custom the services needed to be fast and comfortable, which meant, in practical terms, that the steamers must be able to sail at all states of the tide, and that the train must be able to run close alongside the steamer in order to facilitate quick and easy transfer from one to the other. These two requirements led to the development of the long ferry piers which were so characteristic of those British estuaries which have large tidal ranges and shallow, muddy banks. Expensive piers running far out into deep water and capable of taking the weight of trains were constructed at such places as New Holland on the Humber and New Passage on the Severn, and often drew trade from older, less sophisticated routes which were gradually abandoned.

The construction of railway-owned piers was often accompanied by the building of stations, signal-boxes, hotels and even, as in the case of New Holland, whole villages. On the deeper estuaries wharves or ramps were built instead of piers, but in all cases the railway ferries were of great importance. Links of this kind were established across the Forth, Severn, Tay, and other rivers, and remained a necessity until replaced by bridges.

The only serious attempt to avoid the inconvenience of transferring passengers or goods from train to ship or *vice versa* took place on the Rivers Tay and Forth, where the Granton to Burntisland and Tayport to Broughton Ferry routes employed a number of curious double-ended train ferries whose flush decks were capable of taking two lines of railway stock. These ships had twin funnels set athwartships, rudders at each end, and two engines – one driving each wheel. The *Leviathan*, built in 1849, was the first train ferry in the world, and together with her fleet mates, was disposed of after the opening of the second Forth bridge in 1890.

Rationalisation of the type outlined above did not affect the smaller up-river ferries in the same way. On the Tyne, Thames and Mersey the trade in foot passengers was so enormous that huge fleets of ferries were kept fully employed throughout the Victorian and Edwardian periods, whilst the more rural ferries often formed vital and heavily-used links in an otherwise fairly primitive transport network. Some, like the Cardiff–Penarth ferry, which was designed to carry workers from the city to their place of work in the new docks on the opposite bank of the river, were driven out of existence by the construction of subways or bridges, but others, like the Southampton–Hythe and Dartmouth–Kingswear station connections, survived the Edwardian period and are still in use today.

Finally it should be noted that many small ferries bore a strong resemblance to the river steamers which maintained linear services along the same rivers. Indeed the two roles frequently overlapped and a single steamer fulfilled both functions. In such cases the decision to place individual vessels, such as those of the Tyne General Ferry Company, in this chapter as opposed to the preceding one, is somewhat arbitrary.

35 Built for the Wallasey Local Board's ferry fleet in 1862, the *Heatherbell* was the first Mersey ferry to be fitted with twin funnels, or to have deck saloons fore and aft. With a gross tonnage of 205 tons, she was capable of carrying 807 passengers across the Mersey and was for many years considered to be the 'crack' steamer of the Wallasey fleet. In 1891 she was sold and renamed *Erin's King*, under which name she ran excursion sailings from Dublin for the next nine years. Notice how the helmsman in his 'wheelbox' is positioned between the funnels, whilst the Captain is conning the ship from a separate wooden enclosure on the paddle box

36 Liverpool Landing stage on a busy summer's afternoon during the 1880s. The crowds of intending passengers are waiting to board one of the Wallasey ferries – probably the *Heatherbell* again, although possibly one of the later but similar trio, *Sunflower*, *Daisy* and *Primrose* – by way of a mechanical gangway. Moored further along the stage is the pioneer luggage boat *Oxton*, built for the Birkenhead Improvement Commissioners in 1879 and powered by two sets of twin screws, one set forward and one aft. Unlike the passenger ferries, the luggage boats had no saloons, their large, uncluttered decks being left clear for vehicles

37 LEFT Seen here leaving Southampton is the double-ended, 63-ton *Hampton* which maintained the Southampton to Hythe ferry service from May 1894 until the autumn of 1936. Built by Day, Summers & Company of Southampton, this little steamer incorporated two deck saloons – a sunken one at one end for the second-class passengers, and a larger one, surmounted by a small promenade deck, at the other for the first-class – both lit by paraffin. She carried 214 passengers at 10½ knots

38 LEFT, BELOW The Dutch-built *Tilbury* of 1883, was the last paddler constructed for the London, Tilbury and Southend Railway's service between Tilbury and Gravesend. Until 1893 the route was for passengers only, but thereafter screw ships were introduced and some vehicles carried

39 BELOW This curious outline belongs to another Thames ferry, the *Hutton*, one of three vessels ordered to operate the London County Council's Free Ferry service between North and South Woolwich from 23 March 1889. She and her near sisters *Duncan*, and *Gordon* maintained a regular daily service from 5 a.m. until midnight, at nine-minute intervals, their two independent sets of engines allowing them to crab across the tideway and lay alongside the pontoons with startling efficiency. With their enormous beam (42 ft compared with a length of 164 ft) they were able to carry large numbers of passengers and vehicles. Embarkation was by way of hydraulic ramps which were lowered into place from the pontoons and fitted snugly into gaps provided in the ships' bulwarks. The original ships were replaced during the 1920s and 30s by a quartet of larger but equally bizarre vessels which continued to waddle their way to and fro across the river until they too were broken up during 1963

40 LEFT The train ferry *Carrier* moored at Granton whilst employed on the Edinburgh, Perth & Dundee Railway Company's service across the Forth between Granton and Burntisland, before the completion of the famous bridge. Built in 1858, she was the third train ferry in a series of four built for the company between 1849 and 1861. Each paddle wheel had its own engine and boiler, a rudder was fitted at each end, and she was able to carry two lines of railway waggons on her flat deck. The distance between the two sets of lines was equal to the gauge of the railway stock, so that when traffic was light a single line of waggons could be carried along the ship's centre-line. In 1884 she was purchased by the Isle of Wight Marine Transit Company, and operated a train ferry service between Langstone Harbour and St. Helens, Isle of Wight, from 1885 until withdrawn in 1888. On the far side of the jetty in this picture is the *John Stirling*, one of the N.B.R.'s large passenger ferries, which coincidentally also went south later in her life and operated along the Sussex and Hampshire coasts

41 LEFT The Isle of Wight's first roll-on, roll-off ferry. This little vessel, the *Victoria*, was the first steamer built by Wigham, Richardson & Company at their Neptune Yard, and was launched in July 1860 for a ferry service to Ryde, I.O.W. She was fitted with a hingeing, watertight stern door which enabled cattle, carts, etc., to be driven on board and transported across the Solent without recourse to the dumb barges which were towed behind many of the passenger steamers of the day for that purpose

42 ABOVE Vessels of the Tyne General Ferry fleet laid up at the company's St. Peters repair yard on 18 October 1909. In the centre of the photograph is the *Eleanor*, one of their class B boats. The company's passenger services along the river were quite extensive, and not limited to single-route ferry working; a fact that accounts for the relatively long, lean appearance of their ships

50

43 LEFT A conventional Isle of Wight steamer, the *Duchess of Kent* with her low fo'c'sle and deck saloon aft was typical of local ferries and excursion ships throughout the period 1880–1950. Whilst leaving Portsmouth on one of her regular sailings to Ryde on 3 September 1909, she was in collision with the collier *Transporter* and was badly holed on her port side just forward of the bridge. As the collier backed off, the paddler began to take water so freely that her master had no option but to beach her on Southsea beach, near Victoria Pier, where this photograph was taken. Her 400 passengers were landed safely by boat. Fortunately the accident took place near the top of the tide, and within two days temporary repairs were effected and the steamer floated off. She was sold by the railway in 1933 and saw further service on the Medway and at Blackpool as an excursion ship, before departing for the breaker's yard in 1937

45 BELOW The ferry service from Lymington to Yarmouth, I.O.W. began in 1830, and passed into the hands of the L. & S.W. Railway in July 1884. This photograph shows the *Solent* of 1902 winding her way down the Lymington River with a dumb-barge in tow. Vehicles, livestock and cargo were carried in this precarious manner for many years, as the steamers themselves were designed for passengers only. Although the towing of barges slowed the steamers down and brought complaints from the travelling public, that arrangement must have been preferable to the one which prevailed in bad weather, when the contents of the barge were crammed on board the steamer. Up to 1918 the passenger service was extended from Yarmouth on to Totland Bay all the year round, and to Alum Bay during the summer months up until 1914. The *Solent* lasted until 1948, when she was sold and suffered the ignominy of being beached beside a main road just outside Portsmouth, and converted into Bert's Transport Café

44 LEFT The *Duchess of Edinburgh*, one of the L & SW and L.B. & S.C. Railways' Joint Fleet of Isle of Wight ferries, hurrying away from Ryde pier en route for Portsmouth on a blustery summer's day. She and her sister the *Duchess of Connaught* (known locally as the Ugly Sisters!) departed from the norm of I.O.W. steamer design by having double-ended hulls and twin funnels set athwartships. For all their odd looks, they were strong, reliable steamers which stood up well to the open-sea conditions which were often experienced in Spithead. She lasted for 26 years, and was finally broken up in 1910

Ocean-Going Paddle Steamers

46 An exceptionally rare photograph of Valparaiso harbour in 1852. Anchored in the foreground is the Pacific Steam Navigation Company's wooden paddle steamer *Chile*, of 1840. On 14 September 1840, *Chile* and her sister ship *Peru* were the first steamships to enter the Pacific Ocean, and subsequently operated the long coastal service from Callao to Valparaiso. This photograph illustrates the relative rarity of steamships on the world's oceans at that time

47 An enlarged section of the previous photograph, showing some details of the *Chile's* design. The ship had a clipper bow, square stern, long raised poop deck and vast paddle boxes. For the passage out from England the ship carried a heavier sailing rig than that illustrated here, together with naval pattern 'safety boats' which were carried in an upturned position on the paddle boxes

In comparison with coastal and short-sea vessels, the fully-powered ocean-going paddle steamer was slow to develop, and once established enjoyed only the briefest of ascendancies before giving way to the screw steamer after only half a century on the world's oceans.

Early attempts at steam-powered ocean navigation were bedevilled by two great technical problems. Firstly, the primitive marine engines of the day were grossly inefficient and used prodigious amounts of coal. The famous *Savannah*, for example, had a single-cylinder engine and low-pressure copper boiler which took up most of her hold space and rendered her totally uneconomic as a cargo ship. When she made her famous Atlantic crossing in 1819, even the 75 tons of coal and 125 cords of wood that she was able to carry were insufficient to sustain her boiler for more than short periods in steam, and most of the crossing was made under sail. By the time she raised the Irish coast after 27 days at sea, her log book contained the eloquent entry: 'No cole to git up steam.'

Like the *Savannah*, other early steamers were unable to carry enough fuel to keep their boilers fed, but later vessels, like the Canadian *Royal William* of 1831, were fitted with larger bunkers and more efficient side-lever engines, a combination which might easily have overcome the problem but for the second technical hitch – the design of their boilers. Until Samuel Hall perfected his surface condenser in 1834, all marine boilers were fed by sea water and suffered severe damage unless blown down and de-scaled on every fourth day or so at sea. This tedious operation took about 26 hours, during which time the ship would proceed under sail alone. Thus, although the *Royal William* succeeded in crossing from Nova Scotia to Cowes in the summer of 1833, and her coal supply of 324 tons lasted for the 25-day passage, her periods under sail meant that, in common with the other North Atlantic pioneers, she was in practice an auxiliary steamer.

It was, therefore, the combination of the side-lever engine and the surface condenser which finally made a crossing of the Atlantic under sustained steam power a reality. In April 1838 the 703-ton *Sirius* arrived at New York after an 18-day crossing from Cork, to complete the first true steam crossing. She was followed a few hours later by Brunel's *Great Western*, which had made an even faster passage, crossing from Bristol in 15 days. After that many new steamers began to appear on the Atlantic. Official recognition of their efficiency was forthcoming in November 1838 when the Post Office invited tenders for the carriage of H.M. mails from the British Isles to Nova Scotia, by wooden steamers of not less than 300 H.P.

The successful tender was received from Samuel Cunard, and led to the formation of the British and North American Steam Ship Company Ltd., better known as the famous Cunard Line. The company's first new ships were the *Britannia*, *Acadia*, *Caledonia* and *Columbia*, whose profiles established the norm for subsequent British paddle liners. Built of wood, the ships had three masts, square sterns, clipper bows, and one funnel abaft the paddles. They were fitted with side-lever engines constructed by Robert Napier, and steamed at an average speed of 8 knots. *Brittania* made her first crossing in July 1840, broke all speed records, and promptly claimed the 'blue riband of the Atlantic'.

Although they were larger, faster and more reliable than the average sailing packet on the North Atlantic run, these early paddle steamers must have been very uncomfortable by present day standards. Charles Dickens crossed in *Britannia* in 1842 and has left a lively and illuminating account of his experiences in *American Notes*.

Joining the ship at Liverpool, Dickens found that the accommodation bore precious little resemblance to that represented in 'the highly varnished lithographic print' which hung in the agent's London office. His stateroom he described as an 'utterly impracticable, thoroughly hopeless, profoundly preposterous box . . . than which nothing smaller for sleeping in was ever made except coffins', it being 'no bigger than one of these Hackney cabriolets which have doors behind, and shoot their fares out like sacks of coals upon the pavement.' Of the ship's saloon he thought little better: 'A long, narrow apartment, not unlike a gigantic hearse with windows in the sides; having at its upper end a melancholy stove . . . while on either side, extending down its whole dreary length, was a long, long table over each of which was a rack, fixed to the low roof, and stuck full of drinking-glasses and cruet-stands (which) hinted dismally at rolling seas and heavy weather.'

Heavy weather there certainly was! On the west-ward passage *Britannia* encountered gale-force head-winds, had her paddle boxes demolished and several of her boats destroyed in their davits. Not surprisingly, these events made a considerable impression: 'I say nothing of what may be called the domestic noises of the ship, such as breaking glass and crockery, the tumbling down of stewards, the gambols, overhead, of loose casks and truant dozens of bottled porter, and the very remarkable and far from exhilarating sound made by seventy passengers who were too ill to get up to breakfast. . . . Of the outrageous antics performed by that ship next morning which made bed a practical joke, and getting up, by any process short of falling out, an impossibility; I say nothing.' The hardships of the voyage established at least one fact firmly in Dickens's mind; that 'hot roast pig and bottled ale as a cure for seasickness . . . decidedly failed'!

The Cunard steamers met with considerable competition on the North Atlantic service. The American Collins Line, the Galway Line, the Vanderbilt Line and others joined in the fray, and forced Cunard to build larger and faster vessels. The last wooden Cunarder was the 938 H.P. *Arabia*, which was completed at Greenock in 1852 and lasted on the service until 1864, when she was sold and converted to sail.

The first iron paddler appeared on the Atlantic in 1855 in the form of Cunard's beautiful *Persia*. Built by Robert Napier of Glasgow, the ship was 398 ft long, 3300 tons, and was divided into seven watertight compartments. Her powerful engines drove her at 13 knots and enabled her to hold the 'blue riband' until 1862.

Few metal-hulled paddle steamers were built for the Atlantic ferry. In addition to *Persia*, there were the Galway Line's *Pacific* of 1854 and *Connaught* of 1860; the French Line's eight vessels built between 1863 and 1865; Brunel's screw- and paddle-powered leviathan *Great Eastern*, and Cunard's final paddler, the *Scotia* of 1861. The latter ship was generally similar to *Persia* and came from the same builder. She was, however, slightly larger and more powerful and soon wrested the 'blue riband' from her quasi-sister. Of 3871 gross tons with a hull measuring 400 ft × 47 ft 8 in × 20 ft, she was fitted with the usual side-lever engines, and attained 16.5 knots on trials. Steam was provided by eight tubular boilers with 40 furnaces, the fuel consumption being in excess of 180 tons per day.

Scotia was the last and finest paddle steamer to sail on the Atlantic ferry. She made her final trip for Cunard in September 1875, and was subsequently sold and converted into a twin-screw cable ship. It was in that guise that she was finally wrecked at Guam in the Ladrone Islands in 1904.

Although the North Atlantic ferry was the best-known and most prestigious liner route, it was not the only one to use paddle steamers. By 1840 the Royal Mail Line had obtained a contract to carry mails from Britain to the West Indies, and built a fleet of 14 paddlers, all named after British rivers and estuaries, to maintain the service. Operating originally from Falmouth and later Southampton, paddlers lasted on the mail run until finally ousted by screw vessels in the 1860s.

By 1835, the Peninsular S.N. Company was operating steamers to Spain, and having changed its name to the Peninsular and Oriental S.N. Company, continued to add paddle vessels to its fleet until 1850, by which time the company's routes extended as far east as India and Hong Kong. The last two paddlers on the P & O's Mediterranean services, the *Syria* and *Nyanza* were not withdrawn until 1864.

In 1840, two wooden, 700-ton paddlers belonging to the Pacific Steam Navigation Company, incorporated by Royal Charter in February 1840, had the distinction of being the first steam vessels to round Cape Horn and enter the Pacific Ocean. The *Chile* and *Peru* were built at Limehouse in 1840, and after running trials on the Thames, set off for South America. The *Chile* left Falmouth on 27 June and was followed by her sister, from Plymouth, on 15 July. Both ships carried passengers and cargo, and proceeded under steam and sail to Rio de Janeiro, whence they sailed in company on 30 August, passing through the Straits of Magellan and arriving at Port Famine on 14 September. After taking on wood and water the ships hoisted the Chilian flag and sailed northwards, finally entering Valparaiso amidst scenes of great festivity, on 15 October.

The ships then settled down to operate a regular service between Valparaiso and Callao, at that time the longest steamship route in the world. The company subsequently extended its activities to include a large variety of long routes on the West coast of South America, and finally introduced the first direct U.K.–West Coast service in 1868. The vessels employed on these sailings were the 1631 ton quartet of paddlers *Santiago*, *Limena*, *Panama* and *Pacific*, all built by John Elder in 1865.

The achievements of the PSNC are all the more remarkable when one considers the practical implications of operating early steamers on long routes, far from the repair facilities and coal supplies available at home. On 31 May 1841 the *Chile* struck a reef and reached Valparaiso in a sinking condition, 2,300 miles from the nearest port where adequate repairs could be made. In order to save the ship, Captain Peacock had no option but to remove her engines, shore up the boilers, caulk in all the apertures in her hull, haul the ship down onto her beam ends, and replace the damaged planking himself. Of this amazing feat he wrote: 'I believe that this is the first steamer that was ever hove down, at least with the keel out, and I think that I would scarcely venture to heave down another.'

Supplying coal to steamers in overseas ports was fraught with difficulties. Sailing ships were used to carry coals out from England, and to establish coaling stations on steamer routes: clearly an expensive and laborious business. The inventive Captain Peacock went one step further and used his coasting steamers to prospect for coal seams! On the voyage out from England the *Chile* and *Peru* had refilled their bunkers with coal excavated from the cliff-face at Talcahuano, and by the end of 1841 members of the ships' companies had worked over 4,000 tons from a mine established by Peacock. In another attempt to overcome the coal supply problem, the PSNC ordered the *Valparaiso* from Elders in 1856. The ship was fitted with the first effective set of marine compound engines and used 50% less coal than her side-lever running mates. The economies were so startling that the company converted several of its older ships to compound installations, and the shipping world in general began to abandon the outdated side-lever engine.

Naturally, the coal supply problem increased in proportion to the length of the passage a ship was required to make. The voyage from the U.K. to Australia posed enormous difficulties, and it was in an attempt to overcome them that I.K. Brunel first conceived the design for the famous *Great Eastern*. The mammoth 22,000 ton ship was six times bigger than any other ship of the period, and had vast bunkers which would enable her to steam to Australia and back without calling at intermediate coaling stations.

The story of the ship is too well-known to bear repetition here. Suffice it to say that due to the commercial incompetence of her builder, John Scott Russell, the ship's successive owners experienced severe financial difficulties, and the *Great Eastern* never sailed on the route for which she was intended. After the ship was eventually launched in January 1858 she was used as a passenger ship on the North Atlantic Ferry, but proved uneconomical. After various trials and tribulations she was eventually converted to a cable ship, and enjoyed a successful period in that role. Her best-known achievement was the laying of the first successful Atlantic cable in 1866. Not until the launch of the *Lusitania*, 48 years after the *Great Eastern* took to the water, was Brunel's legendary ship exceeded in tonnage. She was finally broken up on Merseyside in 1888, but has remained the best-known, if least representative, ocean-going paddle steamer ever built.

During the American Civil War of 1861–5 another breed of paddle steamer appeared on the Atlantic. In April 1861 the Northern States declared a blockade of the southern ports in an attempt to starve the Confederates of arms and supplies. The blockade also had the effect of depriving the Lancashire cotton industry of its raw materials, so when Confederate agents began to arrive in British ports looking for fast steamers to run the blockade, they found no shortage of willing agents.

The Confederates needed ships which were fast enough to outrun the warships of the blockading squadrons, and the fast cross-channel steamers which were then so common in British waters fitted the bill perfectly. Many such ships were sold and converted to run the blockade, and soon found themselves dodging enemy warships in the waters between Bermuda, the Bahamas and the American coast. As ships were captured or sunk by the Northern gunboats, the supply of spare cross-channel vessels began to run out, and several British yards began to build vessels specifically as blockade runners. One of the best-known builders' yards was that of Messrs. Jones, Quiggin & Company, of Liverpool, who produced such famous ships as the *Banshee* of 1862, and the infamous *Colonel Lamb* of 1864, which caused the Union a great deal of worry both as a successful blockade runner and as a privateer. By the time the blockade was lifted in 1865, most of the fast steamers had either been destroyed or captured and commissioned in the U.S. Navy. One or two, including the *Colonel Lamb* returned to commercial service, or were sold to foreign navies.

48 Cunard's last wooden paddle steamer, the *Arabia*, fitting out in Robert Napier's Glasgow dock, 1853. Although her paddle wheels have not been fitted she is fully rigged, and presents a profile typical of the early wooden mail steamers. Some years later, in 1861, she narrowly avoided a head-on collision with the *Great Eastern* in fog off Cape Race. Had the collision taken place the results might have been appalling since the two liners were carrying a combined load of 3,500 passengers

49 RIGHT The Pacific Steam Navigation Company's *Talca* of 1862, lying at anchor in the Guayas River, Ecuador. Built of iron at Glasgow, the *Talca* was one of the company's secondary fleet of vessels, which served the minor South American ports, and connected with the larger paddlers, which maintained the long coastal services. Like all the company's small steamers, she made the hazardous 8,500 mile voyage out to the west coast under her own steam

50 RIGHT This photograph, taken on 23 May 1871, shows another PSNC steamer, the *Valparaiso*, at anchor off the beach of Isla Tengo, in the Bay of Puerto Montt, Chile. Built in 1856, the *Valparaiso* was the first steam ship to be fitted with a compound steam engine, and on her voyages from Valparaiso to Panama and back burnt only 640 tons of coal, as compared with 1,150 tons used by vessels with side-lever engines. She was wrecked in 1872 on Lagartija Island near Puerto Montt, and as recently as 1977 several items of company crockery were recovered by divers

51 Brunel's *Great Eastern*, lying on her specially constructed gridiron at Milford Haven, *c*.1862. It is probable that this photograph was taken whilst the ship was undergoing repairs following the great gale of 1861, which did £60,000 worth of damage to the ship during one of her Atlantic crossings. The figures standing under her forefoot give some impression of the ship's enormous size

52 A view of part of the balcony in the *Great Eastern's* grand saloon. This sumptuous room was 63 ft long and 47 ft wide, its walls were hung in richly patterned cloth of gold, the funnel casings were clad with mirrors and arabesque panels, and it was lit by massive gilt chandeliers supplied with gas from the ship's own gasometer. This picture shows one of the chandeliers, and gives a fine impression of the Victorian magnificence of the ship's furnishings

53 A deck view on board the *Great Eastern*, taken during her period as a cable ship, *c*.1870. In addition to completing four trans-Atlantic cables, the great ship was responsible for laying the first submarine cable between Aden and Bombay. The grand saloon of the previous picture was stripped of its fittings, and used as a vast cable tank which was capable of holding over 2,000 miles of cable

55 RIGHT G. & J. Burns' cross-channel steamer *Giraffe*, fitting out for blockade running in Tod & McGregor's drydock at Meadowside, Glasgow, in October 1862. Built in 1860 for the Greenock to Belfast service, the *Giraffe* was sold to the Confederates and made several successful trips under the name *Robert E. Lee* before being captured by a Northern gunboat whilst running a load of arms and military clothing. The identity of the ship on the left of the photograph is unknown

56 BELOW, RIGHT Another fast British steamer, the *Juno* of 1860, fitting out in the Kelvin before running the blockade, *c*.1863. On the left of the picture is the Isle of Man Steam Packet Company's *Mona's Isle*, a 339-ton paddle steamer which was converted into a twin-screw steamer in 1883, and renamed *Ellan Vannin*. On 3 December 1909 she foundered near the Liverpool Bar whilst on passage from Ramsey to Liverpool in a force-12 gale with the loss of all her passengers and crew. In the centre of the picture behind *Juno's* stern is the Campbell steamer *Mail*

54 BELOW The first trans-Atlantic iron mail steamer, Cunard's beautiful *Persia*, on the stocks in Robert Napier's Glasgow yard in 1855. The photograph emphasises the ship's sweet lines and magnificent bow, and makes it easy to imagine why she held the 'blue riband' of the Atlantic from 1856 until 1862

57 A hazy but atmospheric shot of Cunard's *Scotia*, the last paddle liner on the North Atlantic. A powerful and elegant ship, she represented the peak of ocean-going paddle steamer design, and her last crossing in September 1875 brought the era to a fitting close

Warships

58 H.M.S. *Dasher* was built in 1837 for the Weymouth–Channel Islands mail service. A wooden steamer of 357 tons, she was typical of the earliest Admiralty packets, most of which had originally been built for and operated by the Post Office. In 1845 *Dasher* was transferred to survey work on the south coast, but returned to the Channel Islands in 1860, this time as a fishery protection vessel. The photograph shows her on the mud in Gorey Harbour, Jersey, which was her base for many years. Note the figurehead of a sailor in a round cap

The British Admiralty at the beginning of Queen Victoria's reign was a conservative, even moribund institution. Following the decisive naval victories of the Napoleonic wars, the Royal Navy's command of the seas had remained unchallenged. The Admiralty had gradually sunk into a state of complacency, content to trust in the continuing efficiency of its well-tried sailing navy and the time-honoured tactics of bringing the enemy to action broadside to broadside.

The Lords of the Admiralty were not totally unmoved by the rapid acceptance of steam vessels into the merchant marine, and in 1816 carried out some trials with the steamers *Congo* and *Regent*. Three years later they hired the *Eclipse* for towing trials on the Thames, but it was not until 1822 (by which time there were 96 steamers totalling 13,125 tons on the British register) that they had the *Comet*, a 238-ton wooden steamer with two 40 H.P. Bolton and Watt engines, built at Deptford. This little ship was used as a maid of all work and proved sufficiently successful to be followed by an assortment of tugs and other special service vessels. She was finally broken up at Portsmouth in 1869.

Their Lordships' acceptance of these new-fangled steamboats was, however, less than enthusiastic. Whereas a merchant shipowner might introduce steam power, risking only the loss of his profits if the innovation was unsuccessful, a similar misfortune within the Navy might have a direct bearing on national safety or prestige. The Admiralty felt, with some justification, that they could not risk the introduction of steampower into the Navy until the efficiency of the innovation had been proved beyond doubt elsewhere. Furthermore, whilst the hulls of the early steamers could be built in the Royal Dockyards on the Thames, the engines had to be designed and constructed by outside contractors who, since the Navy had no corps of steam engineers of its own, were often obliged to supply engine-room staff along with their engines.

This state of affairs persisted until 1830, when Sir James Graham replaced Lord Melville at the Admiralty and a wind of change began to blow through the corridors of Whitehall. Responsibility for designing the new paddle steamers finally passed to the Surveyor to the Navy, but the situation that ensued was not without a certain irony. The Admiralty, having finally capitulated to the march of progress, now entrusted the designing of most of its new paddle warships to Sir William Symonds, a gentleman whose reputation as a naval architect was based upon his undoubted ability to design *sailing* ships! Symonds was responsible for many of the Navy's final generation of sailing men-of-war, and it has been claimed that his designs brought that class of

ship to its highest peak of perfection.

Unfortunately, however, Sir William's designs did not suffer the transformation from sail to steam at all happily. His ships characteristically had exceptionally sharp floors and carried their extreme breadth far above the point of deepest immersion. Whilst this arrangement was satisfactory in sailing ships it was unsuitable in steamers since the resulting hull-form made the positioning of engines difficult. Rather than yield to the demands of his new power source, Symonds initially tended to stick as far as possible to his old principles, with the result that he was forced to reduce the armament of his early ships and keep their engine size and power to a minimum. The result, claimed his critics, was under-powered, under-armed, vulnerable ships. In fairness, however, it must be said that Symond's designs were no worse than those of other designers, and that by the late 1830s a flattening of his floors was noticeable – a development forced upon him by the ever-increasing size of engines. Furthermore, it should be remembered that until the development of the compound engine during the 1870s, steamships were unable to carry enough coal to sustain them on ocean passages and spent the bulk of their time at sea under sail. Perhaps, therefore, Sir William's adherence to the sailing-ship hull-form was not so very much out of place.

This brief introduction, however, is not the occasion for debate on the pros and cons of Symond's designs. Suffice it to say that, whatever his failings, he was responsible for designing the bulk of the major paddle warships over the next decade and a half. The accession of Queen Victoria in 1837 coincided with the completion of his H.M.S. *Gorgon*, a first-class paddle sloop of 1,108 tons, the first product in a major building programme which finally confirmed the acceptance of paddle steamers as Royal Naval fighting ships.

It appears that no paddle ships-of-the-line were ever built, but the mode of propulsion was applied to a

59 RIGHT Built in 1842 at Chatham dockyard, the wooden first-class paddle sloop H.M.S. *Virago* was one of a small force of British ships which was cruising in the Sea of Japan when war with Russia was declared in 1854. The squadron closed the Russian coast, but apart from forcing three enemy warships into harbour and burning several transports, achieved little of significance. *Virago* landed a party of seamen who succeeded in spiking the guns of the battery at Avalska Bay, and later undertook the unhappy task of carrying the body of the squadron commander, Rear Admiral Price, to sea for burial. In this fine photograph *Virago* displays all the characteristics of the early paddle warships. Note particularly her heavy sailing rig and the retention of the 'grand cabin' in the stern

large number of frigates and sloops. The job of classifying paddle warships is a difficult one because over the years the Admiralty changed its official categories several times. In addition, it was not uncommon for individual ships to change status in accordance with the ranks of their captains or the size of their crews.

The ascendency of the paddle was, however, a brief one, lasting little more than ten years. Even as the new paddle frigates and sloops were joining the fleet, great advances were being made in the development of the screw propellor. Indeed, it has been argued that but for the tardiness of the Admiralty to adopt new ideas, the Navy might have missed the paddle era altogether and moved directly from sail to screw propulsion. This comment is not altogether justified since the first practical sea-going screwship in the World, the *Archimedes*, was not built until 1838. The Admiralty hired her for trials and after due consideration ordered its first screw warship in 1842.

Built at Sheerness and named *Rattler*, the vessel was fitted with her machinery in the East India Docks, London, in July 1843, and soon proved to be a great success. In 1845 she underwent a convincing set of trials with the paddle sloop *Alecto*, the former ship beating her opponent over an 80-mile course by $23\frac{1}{2}$ minutes in calm water, and by an even bigger margin

in a moderate sea and a head wind. The trials were concluded by the celebrated tug-of-war in which the *Rattler* succeeded in towing the *Alecto* stern first at a rate of $2\frac{1}{2}$ knots. Although the depth of water over which the trials were run almost certainly favoured the screw, the demonstration was sufficiently conclusive to sound the death-knell of the paddler as a major warship. After 1846 most new, major warships were screw-powered, the Navy's last paddle frigate being the *Valorous* of 1852.

It must be admitted that as warships paddle steamers had always had a number of inherent disadvantages. Their large paddleboxes, sidehouses and sponsons took up a great deal of space and significantly reduced the number of guns they could carry in either broadside.[1] As well as reducing the ships' firepower, the paddleboxes and wheels made excellent targets for enemy shot and, once disabled, most paddlers were miserable sailers, their enormous top hamper, increased windage, and the drag of their paddles making them almost unmanageable.[2]

It is not surprising therefore, that following the *Rattler*'s victory, paddle steamers fell from favour. They continued to be built and to give sterling service for many years, but in rather different roles. Tugs, gunboats, survey ships, yachts and other special-service vessels were constructed in place of the

frigates and sloops of the 1840s and 50s, most of which had been disposed of by the early 1890s. Yachts and other special-service vessels lingered well into the twentieth century, the last paddle vessels, discounting tugs, to leave the Navy List being the river gunboat *Kinsha*, sold in 1921, the ferry steamer *Harlequin* which became a casualty in 1943, and the survey ship *Triton* which remained in active service until 1914. After the First World War she was put on permanent loan to the Gravesend Sea School as a training ship, in which role she survived until October 1961, when she was broken up at Bruges.

The fact that paddle warships enjoyed only a brief period of popularity within the Royal Navy should not be taken, however, as an indication that they were insignificant within the fleet of their day. In April 1859 it is recorded that the Navy possessed 9 paddle frigates, 61 paddle sloops and 11 paddle tenders as compared with 19, 33 and 0 screw ships of each respective type.

These steamers were seldom idle, for the demands of the Empire were many and various, and the fragile Pax Britannica was only maintained by the constant exertions of the armed forces. During Victoria's reign, England was involved in over 200 small wars and punitive expeditions at an average rate of four per year, as well as the major conflicts of the Crimean and Boer wars. It was the former campaign which, more than any other, proved the worth of the paddlers. As soon as war seemed imminent, a large fleet of steamers sailed for the Baltic under the command of Vice Admiral Sir Charles Napier (incidentally one of Symond's most outspoken opponents), and it is recorded that at least 35 paddlers were present. The naval campaign in the Baltic was one of blockade and bombardment in which the superior speed and manoeuvrability of the steamers proved invaluable. Unlike the sailing ships, they were able to dash in, shell enemy positions and escape again before the forts were able to bring their guns to bear. This advantage was offset by the fact that the paddlers carried smaller broadsides than the sailing ships-of-the-line and were therefore unable to inflict as much damage. The problem was overcome by pairing each paddler with a large sailing ship. The paddler, towing ahead or lashed alongside, provided the motive power and the sailing ship the fire power. These tactics were employed with great success during the bombardment of Sebastopol in 1855.

Paddle steamers served in all of the world's oceans and in the majority of the Victorian wars. The shallow draught of the smaller paddlers made them ideal for river and coastal operations; the records showing them hard at work on the Irawaddy during the Burmese wars of 1852 and 1855 and along the coast of Egypt throughout the long struggle over the Sudan.

Chasing slave ships, subduing the pirates in the China seas and policing the South Sea Islands were just a few of the more colourful aspects of the Navy's work during this period, whilst many other ships were employed in more mundane roles as tenders and mail packets in home waters.

In view of the energy with which the Victorians tackled the job of photographing their military campaigns, it is surprising that more photographs of paddle warships do not exist. Sadly, however, they are scarce, for the military photographers of the time seem to have concentrated their attentions upon the technically more simple subject of the army. Certain constraints have thus been placed upon the composition of this chapter, but the selection which follows nevertheless represents, as clearly as possible, the major types of paddle warships which were to be found in the Victorian Navy. Royal Yachts and paddle tugs are dealt with elsewhere in this book.

[1] The following table emphasises the differences in the fire power of screw and paddle warships of approximately the same tonnages:

	PADDLE	SCREW
Frigates	*Retribution* of 1844, 1641 tons, 28 guns.	*Curacoa* of 1853, 1571 tons, 31 guns.
	Valorous of 1852, 1250 tons, 16 guns.	*Dauntless* of 1848, 1547 tons, 25 guns.
Sloops	*Styx* of 1841, 1057 tons, 6 guns.	*Miranda* of 1857, 1039 tons, 15 guns.

[2] Not all were poor sailers. The *Punjauo*, built in India for the Indian Navy, had a reputation as a fast ship. Later, when sold out of the service, her machinery was removed and she became the clipper *The Tweed*. The story is told that her lines formed the basis for the *Cutty Sark*.

60 The quarterdeck of the second-class sloop H.M.S. *Argus* of 1849, again illustrating the similarity in design between the early steamers and their sailing counterparts. *Argus* was a well-travelled ship: after spending her early life in the Mediterranean she fought in the war with Japan (1862–5), contributed men to the Abyssinian expedition of 1868, and was heavily engaged in the Ashantee War of 1873

61 A group of bluejackets around one of H.M.S. *Argus's* upper deck guns. She was armed with six muzzle-loading pieces of this type, and carried a complement of 175 officers and men

62 H.M.S. *Firequeen* was an iron steamer originally built for the Honourable East India Company in 1845, but purchased by the Admiralty in 1847. She spent most of her life in Indian waters, and took an active part in the Second Burmese War of 1852–3, her shallow draft making her particularly useful during the campaign on the Irawaddy. Later in her career she served as the Port Admiral's yacht at Portsmouth, and was finally broken up in 1883

63 H.M.S. *Valorous* was the last paddle frigate built for the Royal Navy. She sailed in Napier's fleet to the Baltic, and spent the early months of the war with Russia as one of Rear-Admiral Plumridge's detached squadron of paddlers, harassing enemy shipping and shore positions in the Gulf of Bothnia. Later, whilst engaged in the blockade of Bomarsund, the chief fortress of the Aland Islands, she had cause to live up to her name. The paddle frigate *Penelope* had grounded under the guns of the fort and was being badly damaged by red-hot shot, but *Valorous* together with the paddlers *Hecla*, *Gladiator* and *Pigmy* steamed in under heavy fire and succeeded in towing her to safety. *Valorous* took part in the defence of Eupatoria, the bombardment of Sebastopol, and finished the campaign as Rear-Admiral Stewart's flagship at the fall of Kinburn. She was sold out of Naval service in February 1891

4 H.M.S. *Enchantress* was completed in 1865 as H.M.S.
Ielicon, one of a class of fast wooden dispatch vessels.
he served in a variety of roles and campaigns until
888, when she was renamed *Enchantress* and converted
to an Admiralty yacht. In that guise she had the
onour of carrying Queen Victoria at the official opening
f the Manchester Ship Canal in May 1894

65 LEFT Seen here at anchor in Weymouth Bay, H.M.S. *Lively* was a sister ship to the *Helicon*. She was built at Sheerness dockyard in 1870, and wrecked off the coast of Stornoway on 7 June 1883, fortunately without loss of life. Her bow form, sometimes referred to as a 'plough', added six feet to her waterline and in addition to reducing the amount of pitching as compared with those of her sisters not similarly fitted, gave her just over an extra knot in speed

66 BELOW This view of Malta's Grand Harbour was taken between the years of 1893 and 1896. The vessel in the foreground is H.M.S. *Cockatrice* and moored ahead of her is the Admiralty tug *Samson*. Built in 1880 as the *Niger* but renamed in 1881, the *Cockatrice* was one of a class of special-service vessels. Although sometimes known as gunboats, these ships were lightly armed, carrying only two 20 pdr. breach-loading guns. Before coming to the Mediterranean the *Cockatrice* served on the Danube, and in 1896 was again re-named – this time as H.M.S. *Moorhen*

67 LEFT Constructed by R. & H. Green of Blackwall in 1882, H.M.S. *Sphinx* was a naval survey ship. She spent most of her life carrying out her exacting but peaceful duties, but her armament of one 6 in and six 4 in guns made her a force to be reckoned with in times of war. She was attached to the Red Sea Division of the Mediterranean fleet at the time of the abortive struggle against the Mahdists in the Sudan, and contributed to the Naval Brigade which marched under General Graham to relieve the beleaguered garrison at Tokar. *Sphinx* was finally sold in 1919 at Calcutta

68 Seen here during her period as Port Admiral's yacht at Devonport, the rakish iron steamer H.M.S. *Vivid* was originally built at Chatham in 1848 for the cross-channel packet service operating from Dover. In 1854, when the service was handed over to commercial interests, she became tender to the *Fisgard* on the Thames, moving to Devonport in 1873 when she became tender to the *Royal Adelaide* and Port Admiral's yacht. From 1887 she was placed on the sales list and replaced by a screw yacht of the same name, finally being sold a year later

Royal Yachts

69 H.M.Y. *Elfin* – 'the Milk Boat' – leaving Portsmouth on one of her regular morning sailings with the dispatches from London. Later in her career a shelter was fitted to the bridge, but in this early view the captain, resplendent in his cocked hat and frock coat, stands exposed to the elements

Although they flew the White Ensign and were manned by naval crews, the Royal Yachts of Victorian and Edwardian England were rendered so distinctive both by their outward appearance and by the traditions which surrounded them that they demand a chapter of this book to themselves. Furthermore, the sub-order which concerns us here – the paddle yachts – enjoyed a period of employment which almost exactly parallelled the reign of Queen Victoria, and can thus perhaps be regarded as being more essentially Victorian than any other type of paddle vessel.

Before Victoria's accession to the throne, the British monarchy had maintained a variety of yachts which were generally employed on naval duties when not required for Royal service. All these yachts had been sailing vessels, and Victoria inherited the last of them, the *Royal George*, which had been built in 1837 for the Prince Regent. Outwardly this aging vessel was a sober, traditional, three-masted ship, but the dignified exterior concealed an interior whose extravagance and splendour has been compared with Brighton Pavilion.

The young Queen made only one trip in the *Royal George*, from Woolwich to Leith in 1842, but was apparently not amused either by the interior decor or by the length of the passage. The old ship took three days to complete the voyage, and the Queen returned home in a chartered paddle steamer. It appears that this time she was favourable impressed, for within three months, on 7 November 1842, the keel of the first Royal paddle yacht was laid down at Pembroke Dock.

Named *Victoria & Albert*, the new yacht was commissioned on 1 July 1843 and met with the Queen's immediate approval. Victoria, it seems, had a great affection for the sea and ships, and over the years became extremely attached to her successive yachts, making full use of them throughout her reign. Indeed, the services of the Royal yachts were so frequently called for that policy was changed and they were no longer offered to the Navy, but instead spent their brief periods of idleness laid-up.

This continuous Royal service, coupled with the Queen's notorious dislike of change, led to the growth of a number of curious customs and anomalies, many of which have persisted to this day. The Queen disliked noise, so every man in the hand-picked crew wore soft shoes, and spoken orders were kept to a minimum. It is still the case that ratings in the yachts wear white badges on working rig, whilst the rest of the navy wears red, and that uniform jumpers are worn tucked into the trousers, even though the practice was discontinued in the rest of the fleet after dress regulations were changed round the turn of the century.

When Captain J.R.T. Fullerton of the second

Victoria & Albert was promoted to Rear-Admiral in 1893, another curious situation arose. In the normal course of events no officer of flag-rank took personal command of his ship, but in Fullerton's case Victoria made an exception. Unwilling to lose his services, but anxious to see him promoted, the Queen created the post of Flag Officer commanding Royal Yachts, appointed Fullerton to it, and insisted that he retain command of the yacht. The practice has persisted, and in the Navy of today the Royal Yacht *Britannia* is the only ship personally commanded by a Rear-Admiral.

The first *Victoria & Albert* was a wooden vessel of 1,034 tons. In comparison with her successors she was not a beautiful vessel; her high freeboard, massive paddle boxes and single bell-topped funnel gave her a rather ungainly profile. Nevertheless, she was a stately ship and well-liked by the Queen. In view of the Admiralty's reticence to trust in paddles as the primary power source for the fighting ships of the day, it is interesting that the *Victoria & Albert* did not carry a full sailing rig in the manner of contemporary warships. Instead she was given two pole masts and trusted completely in the reliability of her engines. As it turned out, the Admiralty's confidence was justified, and she proved to be a reliable and speedy ship.

The *Victoria & Albert* remained the principle Royal yacht for 12 years, during which time she carried the Queen on more than 20 voyages to the Continent and around the British coast. The possession of a comfortable floating home enabled the Queen to visit such remote areas as the west coast of Scotland and north Wales, which, due to the bad state of the roads and the non-existence of the railway network, had been inaccessible to previous monarchs. The yacht was accompanied on her cruises by the smaller screw-tender *Fairy*, whose length of 146 ft and beam of 21 ft enabled her to cruise in shallow, coastal waters and land the Queen in small ports where the larger yacht could not venture.

In 1849 a third Royal yacht was commissioned. This was the little single-funnelled *Elfin*, which was built specifically to serve the new Royal residence at Osborne House on the Isle of Wight. The Queen had bought the house from Lady Isabella Blatchford shortly after visiting the Island during one of the *Victoria & Albert*'s first cruises in 1843, and now required a shallow-draft yacht which could be constantly available to convey members of the Royal household between Osborne and the mainland. Whenever the Queen was in residence on the Island the *Elfin* left Portsmouth daily at 10 a.m. with the dispatches from London, putting in a return trip to Southampton to land the Queen's messenger during the afternoon, and laying overnight at Cowes before sailing for Portsmouth again early next morning. In this manner she became very much a part of the local scene, her regular habits earning her the affectionate sobriquet 'the Milk Boat'. Fittingly the little yacht was broken up in 1901, shortly after the death of her owner.

In 1855 the first *Victoria & Albert* was renamed *Osborne* and replaced as principal Royal Yacht by the second *Victoria & Albert*. The new ship was considerably larger than her predecessor, measuring 300 ft × 40 ft 3 in with a displacement of 2,470 tons, compared with the older ship's 1,034, and was a result of considerable discussion within the Admiralty. At a time when the paddle was being ousted by the screw propellor in all other branches of the Navy, it might be supposed that their Lordships would have provided the Queen with a modern, fashionable screw yacht. This, however, was not to be, for after lengthy discussions it was decided that speed and efficiency must be sacrificed for the comfort of the Queen. Paddle steamers, it was claimed, were better sea-boats, rolled and vibrated less, and due to their shallow draft were able to keep closer to the coast and visit more ports than their screw counterparts. Tradition won and the new yacht appeared as a wooden paddle steamer.

Conservative or not, the new *Victoria & Albert* was undeniably beautiful. Designed by Sir Oliver Lang and built at Pembroke Dock, her fine lines, two well-raked funnels and three masts imbued her with exactly the right mixture of dash and dignity required by the principal Royal yacht. Furthermore, she turned out to be an excellent seaboat, which was no small advantage in view of the Queen's tendency to sea sickness.

The second *Victoria & Albert* soon established herself as the Queen's favourite ship and was used so heavily that she had as much claim to be regarded as a royal residence as any of the palaces ashore. Her Royal apartments contained everything necessary to turn her into a practical, comfortable, floating home, and were regarded with special affection by the Queen owing to the fact that all the interior decorations were designed personally by the Prince Consort.

By 1863 the old screw-tender *Fairy* was showing signs of age and becoming unreliable. In view of the increasing amount of time Victoria spent at Osborne after the death of Prince Albert, it was essential to have a comfortable, reliable yacht which could carry her to and from the island at all states of the tide. None of the larger yachts fitted the bill, so a new paddler was constructed. Named *Alberta* her shallow draft of 7 ft enabled her to berth alongside Trinity Pier at East Cowes even at low water, and her high speed allowed her to keep up with the *Victoria & Albert* during Royal cruises along the coast.

A final paddle yacht was built in 1870. Made of wood like all her predecessors, she bore a very strong resemblance to the *Victoria & Albert*, although she was rather smaller. Named *Osborne*, she replaced the older yacht of the same name, which had finally been scrapped in 1868 after an active life of 35 years. She was used mainly by the Prince of Wales who cruised extensively in the Mediterranean, and was always on board her at Cowes during August.

The death of Queen Victoria on 22 January 1901 also effectively marked the end of the paddle-yacht era. It seems fitting that the *Alberta*, which had so often carried the Queen to her favourite retreat on the Isle of Wight, was chosen to convey her body on the last crossing of the Solent and that the procession of ships that escorted the coffin to the mainland should include the *Osborne* and the *Victoria & Albert*. The latter ship carried the new King and Queen, but as soon as the Royal party disembarked at Portsmouth she was laid up and never sailed again as principal Royal Yacht. She was replaced five months later by the third *Victoria & Albert*, this time a screw ship.

As already mentioned, the little *Elfin* was broken up, and the *Osborne* fell gradually into disuse as the new King forsook her for the new principal Royal yacht. After remaining laid up at Portsmouth for some years she was eventually sold in 1908, leaving only the *Alberta* to linger on through Edwardian times. By 1912 she too was redundant and was broken up at Portsmouth, so bringing to an end the line of Royal paddle yachts whose distinctive and graceful appearance had been so essentially Victorian.

70 ABOVE The first *Victoria & Albert* of 1843. The date of this photograph is uncertain, but it seems likely that it was taken after the ship was renamed *Osborne* in 1855

71 BELOW This fine portrait of the second *Victoria & Albert* emphasises her beautiful lines and the enormous dignity of her profile. The photograph is unusual in that none of the ship's boats are in their davits, and she appears to be flying the red ensign. In all probability the view was taken in 1855, before the ship was commissioned

72 The rakish *Alberta* of 1863 hurrying out of Cowes into the Solent with members of the Royal household on board. A group of gentlemen in top hats may be seen on the fo'c'sle, whilst the ladies are gathered under the awning spread between the funnels. Safe from the eyes of his superiors, if not the camera, one of the ship's cooks is taking his ease at a window on the starboard sponson

73 Built in 1870, the second *Osborne* was used during the summer months by the Prince of Wales, and spent the winter laid up at Portsmouth

74 ABOVE, RIGHT Members of the Royal family, friends, and ship's officers on board the *Osborne* in 1880. Albert Edward, Prince of Wales, is seated in the centre of the photograph, wearing medals. To his left, seated on the steps, are his sons Prince Albert Victor and Prince George

75 RIGHT One of the Royal bedrooms on board the *Osborne*. The photograph was taken in 1877

Cross-Channel Paddle Steamers

76 Sitting on the mud in the tidal harbour at St. Peter Port, Guernsey, is the *Queen of the Isles*, an 81-ton steamer built in 1853 for the mail service between Guernsey, Alderney, Jersey and Cherbourg. With her clipper bow, figure head and bell-topped funnel she was typical of many early packet steamers

On 17 March 1816, the pioneer Thames steamer *Margery*, having been forced off the river by the opposition of the Thames watermen, sailed from Newhaven to Le Havre, and thus became the first steamship to cross the English Channel. She was followed later the same year by the *Defiance* en route to Veere, and on 15 October 1817 by James Watt's 94-foot *Caledonia*, which sailed from Margate to Rotterdam and thence up the Rhine.

These early experiments suggested that it would be practical to introduce steamships onto the regular short-sea routes hitherto operated by sailing packets, and it was not long before the challenge was taken up by David Napier of Glasgow. Napier had inherited a foundry business from his father and, fascinated by the new-fangled steamboats, had set about investigating hull- and marine-engine designs. By 1818 his work had come to fruition and his steamer *Rob Roy*, built to his own design by Denny of Dumbarton and engined by himself, had entered service between the Clyde and Belfast. During her first year the sailings were spasmodic, but after undergoing certain alterations during the winter of 1818–9, she returned the following season to offer a regular cross-channel service, the first of its kind in the world.

Napier's endeavours did not end there, for he continued in the ship-owning business, and built the engines for many more famous cross-channel and sea going steamers. The *Rob Roy* having shown the way, 19 other steamers entered the Belfast trade before 1830, and steam was introduced on several other crossings. On 21 July, 1819, the *Waterloo* inaugurated the Liverpool–Dublin route, and by 1822 steamers were sailing between Bristol and Dublin, Holyhead and Howth, and the Clyde and Derry, to be followed during the next ten years by more vessels on an even wider variety of crossings.

The *Rob Roy* achieved another 'first' when she was transferred to the south coast in 1821 and began the first regular service across the Strait of Dover, between Dover and Calais. She made such an impression that she was purchased by the French Government and used to carry the English mail, under the name of *Henri Quatre*. The British Post Office had hitherto carried the mails to Ireland and the Continent in small sailing cutters which, although they operated with as much regularity as possible, were prone to many kinds of delays. The crossing to the Channel Islands from Southampton or Weymouth, for example, might take as little as 12 hours, but bad weather could extend the passage time to several days. In addition it was not unknown for the sailing packets to be captured by French privateers or seized for smuggling.

The arrival of privately-owned steamboats on the cross channel routes therefore posed something of a problem for the Post Office, whose sailing vessels were thoroughly outclassed both in terms of speed, comfort and reliability. Rather than allow the private vessels to carry the mails the Post Office accordingly ordered some steam packets of its own, and set up in competition. In May 1821 their first steamships, the *Lightning* and *Meteor*, were introduced on the Holyhead–Dublin service, and within a few years most of the other mail services had been converted to steam.

Competition on the Irish sea and English Channel continued to grow, and many new routes were opened. The General Steam Navigation Company was formed in 1824 and within a few years was operating steamers on a wide variety of coastal and short sea services from the south-east coast to such ports as Rotterdam, Dieppe, Le Havre, Dunkirk, Hamburg and Ostend. The pattern continued for many years, with more and more ports receiving the attentions of steamships and the smaller private owners tending to give way to larger but privately owned companies. Where these companies came into competition with the Post Office packets it was the latter which invariably came off worse. Time had proved that the management of the Post Office was unfitted for the specialised job of running a fleet of steamships, which had in any case failed to keep up with the improvements that had taken place in the commercially owned vessels, and were yearly becoming less attractive to prospective passengers. Large losses were being made on many routes and eventually, in 1837, the responsibility for the operation of the packets was transferred to the Admiralty. The mail services were somewhat revitalised by the transfer and many new ships were built. Plates 58 and 68 show H.M. packets *Dasher* of 1838 and *Vivid* of 1847 and illustrate the developments in the design of the mail steamers over the next ten years. But the fact still remained that the private operators were better fitted to gauge the demands of the market, and that competition between commercial owners led to better ships, faster crossings and lower fares. The Admiralty therefore began to look to the possibility of contracting out the carriage of the mails to private concerns and during the course of the 1840s and 50s handed over most of its services in that way. In 1845 they withdrew from the Weymouth–Channel Islands route, by 1849 had abandoned the Irish Sea crossings, and in 1854 handed over the Dover station to Messrs. Jenkins & Churchward's English, French & Belgian R.M.S.P. Company.

The 1840s were distinguished not only by the withdrawal of the Crown from cross-channel steamer operation, but also by the growth of the railways. As the tentacles of the railway network spread outwards towards the coast, the railway companies began to look to the possibility of running their own steamers.

The steam train services they provided enabled passengers, goods and mails to be carried swiftly to the ports, so the provision of an equally efficient and regular steamer service to carry them onwards seemed a logical extension. Initially, however, the enabling acts of the railway companies did not include the powers to run steamers, so in the early days the train services were forced to connect with privately-owned steamers. The Great Western Railway, for example, ran trains to Milford where passengers embarked in the steamers owned by Messrs. Ford & Jackson, whilst at Weymouth a similar arrangement prevailed between the GWR and the Weymouth & Channel Islands Steam Packet Company.

Half measures such as these rarely proved satisfactory, however, and the railway companies soon sought to extend their control. In some cases this was done by pouring money into harbour works and other peripheral expenses incurred by the steamer companies, but more usually by forming subsidiary companies or seeking their own running powers. The speed with which the railways were able to force their new enabling acts through Parliament varied tremendously. The Chester & Holyhead Railway was running steamers between Holyhead and Dublin by 1848, as was the London & South Western between Southampton, Jersey, St. Malo and Granville. Other companies took longer, the South Eastern Railway obtaining powers to run from Folkestone in 1854, and the G.W.R. for its various services in 1871. More examples could be quoted, but the significant fact is that by the end of the 1870s the railway companies were in control of the majority of cross-channel and short-sea routes, and that a new era had begun.

Competition between the railway companies was as hot afloat as it was ashore. A traveller intending to cross to Ireland or the Continent could choose from any one of a large variety of routes, and would naturally favour the ones offering the fastest, largest, most luxurious ships, and the most efficient connecting services at either end. Likewise the Post Office would give the mail contracts to the companies who could offer the most speedy and reliable service. Inevitably, therefore, the standards on most routes continued to rise throughout the remainder of the century, and some splendid ships were produced.

Despite the extensive railway expansion into the cross-channel business some notable private companies continued to thrive. In May 1850 the City of Dublin Steam Packet Company took over the mail contract from the Admiralty and defended it against all-comers until 1920. The company's chief route was between Holyhead and Kingstown, and their most notable vessels were the four 'provinces', *Ulster*, *Leinster*, *Munster* and *Connaught*, built in 1860, and far superior to any vessel which appeared on the Irish sea

for many years.

From the Clyde two major private concerns operated to Ireland. In 1826 G. & J. Burns introduced the *Fingal* on a regular service to Belfast, by 1849 had obtained the mail contract, and by the early 1850s had established a monopoly on the crossing. Their fleet of fine paddle steamers was named, very distinctively, after members of the animal kingdom. Their last paddle steamer was the *Adder*, which was built in 1890 for the Gourock–Belfast daylight service and lasted until 1906, when she was sold for further service in South America. A photograph of the *Giraffe*, one of the company's earlier steamers, will be found in the chapter on Ocean Going paddlers (plate 55), and shows her fitting out for blockade running.

The second major company to run from the Clyde was the Laird Line, which operated to Derry and other ports on the north and north-west coasts of Ireland, but which turned over to screw propulsion quite early in the century and is therefore of less interest to us. The Larne & Stranraer Steamboat Company introduced paddle steamers in 1872, and in 1890 and 1892 had a magnificent pair of sisters built by Denny of Dumbarton. These ships, the *Princess Victoria* and *Princess May*, although capable of 20 knots, were the last paddlers on the route, all subsequent vessels being turbine screw steamers.

Two other private companies worthy of mention are the General Steam Navigation Company Limited and the Isle of Man Steam Packet Company. The former, as already noted, operated from the Thames and the south-eastern ports to a variety of continental destinations, and continued to use paddle steamers until the turn of the century. The last two built for the company were the *Swift* and *Swallow* of 1875, which measured 200 ft 5in × 27 ft 2 in × 14 ft 5 in and were built of iron. They were employed on the London–Ostend passenger and cargo service and were broken up in 1902 and 1901 respectively.

The Isle of Man company was formed in 1829 by a group of local businessmen who were so dissatisfied with the steamboats then running to the island that they decided to have their own vessel built. Originally styled the Mona's Isle Company, their first vessel, the *Mona's Isle*, was built in 1830, to be followed by a succession of splendid paddle steamers. By the 1870s some very large, fast vessels were operating on the company's services from Liverpool, Fleetwood and elsewhere to the Isle of Man ports. These included the four-funnelled *Ben-My-Chree* of 1875, and the 260 ft *King Orry*. The company introduced its first screw steamers in 1878 and 1881, but built several more paddle steamers thereafter, the last being the magnificent *Empress Queen* of 1897 which, with a gross tonnage of 2,140 and a length of 372 ft) was the biggest cross-channel paddle steamer in British waters.

The privately owned and the railway ships had certain features in common. Cross-channel steamers were required to maintain exacting schedules all the year round in waters which were prone to extremely bad weather conditions, and they were thus very strongly built. Most of the ships built in the 1880s and 90s had a large freeboard, and had their sponsons set high above the water to avoid choking the paddle boxes as the ship rolled in a seaway. Large saloon windows were notable by their absence, light being admitted to the passenger accommodation through small, strong port-holes. It was usual for the ships to have either flush upper decks, or to be fitted with turtle-backed fo'c'sles which were designed to throw water aside when they were pitching heavily and digging their bows into the seas. The high speeds required dictated powerful engines, and side-lever, oscillating and compound diagonal types all enjoyed periods of popularity. Multiple boilers were often needed to supply steam, so it was common for cross-channel paddlers to have twin funnels, normally set one forward and one aft of the paddleboxes. A few ships, namely the I.O.M.S.P.C's *Ben My Chree* (II), the City of Dublin Company's four 'provinces', and the London, Chatham & Dover Railway's bizarre *Castalia* and *Calais-Douvres* (I) were fitted with four.

Individual companies naturally favoured particular styles, and there were many variations from the general pattern outlined above. The South Eastern Railway, for example, fitted all its ships with anti-quated but charming bell-mouthed funnels, whilst the rival L.C. & D.R. built a number of double-ended vessels, and experimented with ways of reducing sea-sickness by building three unconventional ships which are described in the captions to this chapter. One or two extremely ungainly vessels were built during the period, but it is generally fair to say that by the 1890s the cross-channel paddle steamers had developed into an extremely powerful and beautiful breed of ship.

In 1897, however, an event took place which was to mark the beginning of the end of the cross-channel paddler. At the review of the fleet at Spithead, C.A. Parsons gave a spectacular demonstration of the power of his steam turbine engine when he took his little *Turbinia* at high speed through the lines of the fleet. By 1901 the *King Edward*, the world's first commercially operated turbine ship, had entered service on the Clyde and proved that she could attain higher speeds at lower costs than her paddle-driven competitors. The large cross-channel paddlers were excessively heavy on coal, so the introduction of fast turbine steamers offered great attractions to their owners, and in 1903 the South Eastern & Chatham Railway introduced the turbine steamer *The Queen* on the Dover Straits services. She was an immediate success, and the fate of the paddle steamer was sealed. The older vessels were rapidly replaced by turbines, and even some of the newer ships were destined to enjoy only short lives. The *Mabel Grace*, the last paddle vessel built for the Dover Straits, lasted only from 1899 until 1909, whilst the same company's *Dover*, *Lord Warden* and *Calais* of 1896, although they were both large and powerful, were replaced in 1911. The last paddlers to sail out of Dover were the French vessels, *Le Nord* and *Pas de Calais* – huge ships of over 2,000 tons – both of which left the service in 1923, (the former having been wrecked, and the latter broken up), and the Belgian *Princess Clementine* of 1896, which was broken up in 1928 after several years in reserve.

The largest and most powerful British cross-channel paddle steamer ever built was the Isle of Man SP Company's huge *Empress Queen*. After her intro-duction in 1897 she broke all existing records by crossing from Liverpool Rock to Douglas Head in two hours and 57 minutes, her mighty triple-expansion engine driving her at over 20 knots. It is interesting to conjecture how long this marvellous ship would have lasted in the face of competition from the more economical turbines, had she survived the war. As it was, she was taken into government service in 1915 and whilst employed as a troop ship stranded on Bembridge Ledge, Isle of Wight, and became a total loss, leaving one of her fleet-mates to claim the honour of being the last British cross-channel paddle steamer in regular use. This was the *Mona's Queen* (II) of 1885, a beautifully proportioned, twin-funnelled vessel, which was closely associated with the Fleetwood–Douglas route. After serving as a troop transport during the 1914–18 war, *Mona's Queen* was reconditioned by Cammell Laird and re-entered ser-vice in 1919, to give the company a further ten years' service before she went to the breakers in 1929 – thus bringing to a close the era of the British cross-channel paddle steamer.

77 LEFT Another veteran – the Galloway Steam Navigation Company's *Countess of Galloway* (II) which was built in 1847 to operate between Wigtown, Garliestown, the Isle of Whithorn, Kirkcudbright and Liverpool. She replaced an earlier vessel of the same name and continued in service until 1879, two years after her owners had been taken over by M. Langlands & Sons of Liverpool

78 LEFT The barque *Louisa* (left) and the Bristol S.N. Company's Bristol–Cork packet steamer *Juverna* in Bristol Docks. *Juverna* was a 16½-knot iron steamer which, when built in 1846 at a cost of £26,050, represented a considerable advance on all the previous vessels on the service

79 ABOVE This photograph illustrates the hull-form of the *Malakoff*, which was built in 1851 to John Scott Russell's famous 'wave line' principles. Originally named *Baron Osy*, she was designed for the Antwerp S.N. Company's London–Antwerp service, but was sold back to her builder during the Crimean War, re-named, and converted for use in Government service. In July 1856 she was sold to Ford & Jackson for the Milford service, but was later taken over by the G.W.R., who kept her until she was broken up in 1884. Note the antiquated appearance of the ship, with her raised poop, highly decorated stern, and anchor suspended from a cathead forward

80 A busy scene at St. Peter Port Quay, Guernsey, as cargo (which includes tin baths and bundles of shovels!) is unloaded by porters' barrow from the London & South Western Railway's *Brittany* of 1864. Her sister ship, *Normandy*, was run down and sunk in a thick fog on 17 March 1870, but *Brittany* remained on the services from Southampton to Le Havre and the Channel Islands until broken up in 1900. This photograph is particularly interesting as it shows details of the ship's deck fittings. Note how the bearded Master is standing on the paddle box from where he would con the ship in and out of harbour, whilst the ship's wheel, her twin binnacles and the engine-room telegraph and skylight are positioned between the boxes on the bridge deck

81 RIGHT Rivals to the L & SWR Southampton steamers for the Channel Island trade were the Great Western Railway vessels. Here we see the *South of Ireland* (left) and the *Aquila* (right) in Weymouth Harbour, *c*.1880. The former ship was built in 1867 for Ford & Jackson's Milford–Waterford service, transferred to the G.W.R. in 1872, and sent to Weymouth in 1878. She lasted there for only five years, for on Christmas Day 1883 she was wrecked on the rocks of Worbarrow Bay whilst feeling her way homewards to Weymouth in a thick fog. *Aquila* was an older ship, launched in 1854 for an unsuccessful service from Harwich to Antwerp, but after remaining laid-up for some time came to Weymouth to operate the Weymouth & Channel Islands S.P. Company's services in connection with the G.W.R. In 1889 she was sold to the Plymouth, Channel Islands & Brittany S.S. Company Limited, and later still found her way to the Bristol Channel were she ran excursions. Photo 107 shows her as the *Alexandra* at Ilfracombe Pier in 1895

82 ABOVE The Penzance–Scilly Isles passenger and cargo steamer *Earl of Arran* struck a rock in St. Martin's Neck on 16 July 1872, and was deliberately run ashore on Nornour Island. Her captain, whose certificate was suspended for four months, had been talked into taking a short-cut by one of his passengers, a pilot-boat sailor called Stephen Woodcock. The *Earl of Arran* was originally built for the Ardrossan S.B. Company's service to Arran, but came south in 1871 to join the West Cornwall S.S. Company Limited. Note the ship's cargo derrick and turtle-back fo'c'sle, a feature common to many packets which worked in open waters

84 LEFT The company's second attempt to combat the problem of *mal de mer* took a very different form. The *Bessemer* was an extraordinary vessel with a single, double-ended hull, so that viewed in profile her bow and stern were indistinguishable. Furthermore, her two masts, two funnels, two navigating bridges and two sets of paddle boxes were arranged symmetrically about her centre line so that she strongly resembled the mythical 'pushmepullyou'! Her four paddle wheels were driven by four sets of oscillating engines, and she was capable of 17 knots. The vessel's real claim to fame, however, lay in her famous 'swinging saloon' invented by her namesake, Sir Henry Bessemer. In principle this saloon could be swung by a set of manually operated hydraulic rams, so that as the ship rolled her way across the channel the saloon and its passengers could be kept on an even keel. It was planned to replace the manual operation by a gyroscopic control if the saloon proved successful, but this was not to be. The combination of her curious, low, whale-backed prows and her unsatisfactory hydraulic steering gear made the *Bessemer* extremely unmanageable when entering and leaving port, and after only four years in service she was withdrawn

83 LEFT A cross-channel curiosity: The *Castalia* was one of two experimental vessels built in 1874 and operated by the London, Chatham & Dover Railway in an attempt to reduce the effects of sea sickness on the Dover–Calais route. Built by the Thames Ironworks at Blackwall, *Castalia* had two half-hulls with straight inboard edges, four funnels, and two separate compound diagonal engines, each of which drove one of the paddle wheels which rotated in the 26-foot gap between the hulls. Sadly, the ship was a total failure. Not only was she a very poor seaboat, but she was only capable of 11 knots, so in 1883 she was sold to the Metropolitan Asylums Board, converted into a floating hospital, and moored in Long Reach on the Thames

85 The third bizarre ship constructed for the L.C. & D.R. was the *Calais-Douvres*, built in 1877 by Hawthorne, Leslie & Company of Newcastle. She was another double-ender, but reverted to the catamaran form used in *Castalia*, except that unlike her predecessor she had two complete hulls with a single large paddle wheel positioned between them. Her speed of 13 knots was adequate at first, and her enormous size and novelty made her popular with passengers, but after nine years in service she was withdrawn as too slow. After many years laid up she was sold as a coal hulk. This view was taken on the deck of the *Calais-Douvres* in mid channel and shows her central bridge, three of her four funnels, and one of the deck saloons. Note the trunks heaped on deck to the left of the two smartly-dressed young ladies

86 The beautiful *Connaught* was one of four similar ships built in 1860 to meet the requirements of a new contract made between her owners, the City of Dublin S.P. Company, and the Post Office in 1859 for the carriage of the Irish Mails from Holyhead to Kingtown in less than $3\frac{3}{4}$ hours. Such timing required ships that were capable of $17\frac{1}{2}$ knots in all weathers and at the time severe doubts were expressed in marine engineering circles as to whether this could be achieved. The new ships, *Connaught, Ulster, Munster* and *Leinster* proved themselves more than equal to the task. *Connaught* was a big vessel with a gross tonnage of 1448 and a length of 338 ft. Steam was produced by eight haystack boilers and her huge oscillating engines developed 750 N.H.P. (4600 I.H.P.), driving her at over 18 knots. She was, in short, one of the most outstanding cross-channel ships ever built and was at least 20 years ahead of her time. Her size and speed was not exceeded on the Irish Channel until 1897, and even at Dover no other ship achieved 18 knots until 1880

87 Holyhead Harbour from the Station Hotel, August 1886, showing an impressive array of London & North Western Railway Dublin steamers alongside. They are, from left to right: *Earl Spencer* (*b.*1874 for the Greenore service and purchased by the L & NWR in 1877); *Duke of Sutherland* (*b.*1868); *Duchess of Sutherland* (*b.*1868, or possibly the *Stanley* of 1864); *Admiral Moorsom* (*b.*1860); an unidentified vessel which could be the tender to the Commissioners for Irish Lights, *Alexandra*, or a railway ship with her funnels removed for overhaul; *Eleanor* (*b.*1881); and on the right either the *Lily* or the *Violet* of 1880. In the far distance another vessel is just visible which has not been firmly identified but could be the

Telegraph of 1854 or another company's ship in for repairs

88 The *Cobra* was built in 1889 for G. & J. Burns' daylight passenger-only service from the Clyde to Belfast. She was a handsome ship, but was fitted with a rather unconventional set of compound engines in which the high-pressure cylinder was set horizontally and the low pressure one diagonally. For some reason she did not prove successful and was sold after only one season to the Liverpool and North Wales S.S. Company, who renamed her *St. Tudno*, only to resell her to Hamburg owners a year later. The Germans restored her original name and used her on a service from Hamburg to Heligoland

89 RIGHT The South Eastern Railway's *Mary Beatrice* leaving the old harbour at Folkestone for Boulogne, *c.*1890. She was typical of the SER's rather dainty vessels, all of which had well raked, bell-topped funnels and generally had long turtle-backed fo'c'sles. *Mary Beatrice* was built on the Thames by Samuda Bros. in 1882

90 By contrast the ships of the rival London, Chatham
& Dover Railway were much more sturdy in appearance
and lacked the bell-topped funnels and turtle-backs.
Here we see the 18½ knot *Invicta* of 1882 leaving
Admiralty Pier, Dover before dashing across the
Channel to Calais. The empty boat train stands on the
quay, and in the background is the bulk of the famous
Lord Warden Hotel, which today houses the local British
Rail offices

91 No less than 11 paddle steamers were visible in the original of this splendid photograph of Dover Harbour, taken from the Western Heights in 1892. The four vessels in the foreground are all L.C. & D.R. ships. From left to right they are *Prince* (1864), *Foam* (1862), *Wave* (1863) and *Invicta* (1882). Moored to the far side of Granville Dock is an unidentified vessel, whilst in the distance, from left to right, the following can be discerned: facing inwards is probably the *Breeze* (1863); at anchor is a paddle tug; alongside the Admiralty Pier is one of the Belgian Ostende packets, *Ville De Douvres*, *Prince Albert* or *La Flandre*; and outside the same pier with only the tops of her funnels showing is either the *Victoria* or *Empress* (1886–7) or the second *Calais-Douvres* (1889). The twin, bell-topped funnels behind the warehouses in the middle distance probably belong to one of the early L.C. & D.R. ships like the *John Penn*, (1860); whilst on the extreme right is the bizarre, twin-hulled *Calais-Douvres* of which a deck view has already been included. If the date of the photograph is correct then she must have been laid up for six years since her withdrawal in 1886

103

92 An unusual deck view of the London, Brighton & South Coast Railway's Newhaven–Dieppe paddler *Rouen* of 1888, showing her turtle-back fo'c'sle with its narrow walkway and her sturdy wheelhouse, which was placed on deck rather than on the more usual raised bridge. Note the sail rigged from the foremast. *Rouen* and her sister ship *Dieppe* were constructed to cope with the anticipated increase in traffic for the Paris Exhibition of 1889, and were the last paddle steamers to operate on the Newhaven route. Both were strong, fast ships whose speed of 19½ knots made them well suited to this longer crossing

93 RIGHT On New Year's Day 1899 the L.C. & D.R. and the S.E.R. merged to form the South Eastern & Chatham Railway, and the former Dover and Folkestone fleets were henceforth managed as one unit. This steamer, the *Mabel Grace*, although ordered by the old S.E.R., came into operation after the merger and her appearance was something of a compromise between the styles of the two former fleets. She was an extremely good-looking ship, and is seen here going astern between the piers at Boulogne on one of her regular trips from Folkestone. She was the last British cross-channel paddle steamer built

94 RIGHT The Isle of Man Steam Packet company's *Empress Queen*, built in 1897 and so named to commemorate the jubilee of Queen Victoria, was the largest and fastest paddle steamer ever built for British owners. With a gross tonnage of 2,140, an overall length of 372 ft and massive 1290 N.H.P. three-crank diagonal engines, she was able to carry 2,000 passengers at over 21 knots. In 1915 she was chartered by the government and converted into a troop ship, but on 1 February 1916 she stranded in fog on Bembridge ledge, Isle of Wight,

and became a total loss: a sad end for a vessel which was, in every respect, the last word in cross-channel paddle steamers. Her fleet-mate, the *Mona's Queen* of 1885, survived the war and became the last British cross-channel paddler in regular service, finally departing for the breaker's yard in 1929

Pleasure Steamers

95 The *Prince*, a typical, early flush-decked steamer, was built in 1852 for Captain Joseph Cosens of Weymouth by the famous John Scott Russell of Milwall. Local tradition has it that the little *Prince* was constructed on the landward side of the famous *Great Eastern* and had to be launched through a gap left in the mighty ship's hull for that purpose! Note her boiler clearly visible on deck, and the canvas dodgers round the bulwarks aft which, when unrolled, afforded the passengers a little protection against the wind and spray. After 28 years at Weymouth, *Prince* was sold to Ellett & Matthews of Exmouth and pioneered pleasure sailings along the South Devon coast. Later still she ran from Lee-on-Solent, and was finally hulked in 1897

One of the most essential elements of any Victorian or Edwardian seaside holiday was a trip to sea on a pleasure steamer. Practically every resort boasted a pier or landing stage from which the more venturesome holiday makers could embark for a trip in one of the vast fleet of paddle steamers which maintained the excursion trade round the coast, or along which the more timorous could stroll to watch the arrivals and departures.

Pleasure steamers were the largest single group of paddlers in the years before the First War and were certainly the most extensively photographed, being a symbol of happy summer days by the sea. Each steamer had its own personality, and many attracted bands of supporters who would sail in the vessel season after season in preference to any other ship. Many were also extremely long lived and became part of the scenery of the resorts which they served, adding significantly to the feeling of permanence and security which pervaded pre-1914 Britain. In addition, of course, they provided the most convenient and comfortable way of travelling from one coastal resort to another.

The popularity of the excursion steamers reached its zenith in the years immediately before the First World War, after a steady ascent which had begun back in 1812 when the *Comet* first entered service on the Clyde. Although she and the other early steamboats were designed for purposes other than operating pleasure trips, they naturally excited the interest of the public, who took the opportunity to sail in them whenever possible. As this demand increased the steamboat owners began to advertise occasional excursions in addition to their regular towage and ferry services. By 1823 it was possible, for example, to sail on a day trip round the Isle of Wight from Southampton, to catch a steamer from London to the Kent coast resorts, or to sail on a variety of routes on the Clyde and elsewhere.

This development was assisted by the growth of a new fashion amongst the upper classes for visiting the seaside. During the early eighteenth century the famous inland spa towns such as Harrogate, Bath and Tunbridge Wells had prospered, but after about 1760 they were severely challenged by the fashion for sea bathing. When George III took to the water at Weymouth, he effectively ended the days when the coast was regarded as a dangerous and hostile region inhabited by the coarser elements of society, and started a trend in which the upper classes began to forsake the inland spas and sample the pleasures of the seaside instead. In doing so he had a profound, if unconscious, effect on the future development of British pleasure steamers.

Transport from the cities to the new coastal resorts often posed a problem. The choice lay between the stage coach and the sailing ship; the former being fast and reliable but very expensive; the latter cheap but often uncomfortable, slow and dangerous. The introduction of the steamboat on coastal services from about 1815 onwards provided the ideal solution and generated an increase in traffic to and from the resorts. One problem remained however – that of landing the fashionably-dressed passengers and their baggage safely. At Ryde on the Isle of Wight, for example, passengers were taken by small boats into the shallow water where they were transferred to a waiting horse and cart or were carried up the beach on the back of a porter! Similarly undignified arrangements prevailed elsewhere, and it was not long before public dissatisfaction led to the building of the first seaside piers.

Originally designed as landing stages for the regular steamers, the function of the first piers gradually changed. During the expansion of Britain's railway network in the 1840s and 50s many coastal resorts were linked with the major towns and cities, and steam trains quickly eclipsed the steamboats as the most efficient means of transport to and from the coast. The cheap excursions offered by the railway companies also meant that spending a day by the sea came within the grasp of the middle classes, and the number of visitors to the resorts grew rapidly. The pier companies, having lost much of their regular traffic to the railways, began to stress the pleasures of 'promenading' and sought for customers from the shore rather than from the sea. The steamers which had previously maintained the regular services to and from the cities also changed their emphasis and began to advertise pleasure sailings from the resorts, in place of the old utilitarian services to them. Thus, the coming of the railways was responsible for the development of both the English pleasure pier and the true pleasure steamer.

The earliest wooden steamers were ornate vessels. Clipper bows, bowsprits, quarter galleries, tall bell-mouthed funnels and sailing rigs were common features, but as iron ship-building developed, practical considerations caused fashions to change. The new iron steamers (and the few that were still built of wood during the 1850s) were much more austere in appearance, and bore a strong resemblance to the tugs described in an earlier chapter, except that the passenger steamers tended to be longer, leaner and lower. Clipper bows, although retained by a few owners, gradually gave way to spoon bows or straight stems. Accommodation, such as there was, took the form of lower deck saloons fore and aft, leaving the main deck completely bare except for the engine house and the side-houses amidships. A small bridge deck often spanned the space between the side houses, and formed the roof to the engine space. The early ships were conned from the paddle boxes and steered by a tiller or wheel in the stern, but by the 1850s it was becoming usual to place the wheel in a small wheel-box on the bridge deck. A single funnel was the norm, placed either ahead or astern of the paddles, according to regional taste. As a broad generalisation it is fair to say that the owners on the south and east coasts of England seemed to favour the funnel-aft design, whilst the Clyde offered a much greater variety, with a large number of ships of both types.

The Clyde, indeed, led the field in steamer design throughout the nineteenth century, the hot competition in that area leading to a continuous refinement of design. Many out-dated Clyde vessels later came south and enjoyed a second youth as celebrities in an area whose steamer services were relatively slow to develop.

An example of a typical flush-decked Clyde vessel of the 1860s was the *Marquis of Bute*, built for the famous Captain McLean in 1868. She was fitted with a single diagonal engine and a haystack boiler, and measured 196 ft × 18 ft 1 in × 7ft 3 in, making her considerably larger than a typical south-coast example, Joseph Cosens' *Prince* of 1852 which, although she measured only 128 ft × 13 ft 3 in × 7 ft 6 in, was the largest and finest steamboat on the Wessex coast in her day. Some flush-decked steamers like the ill-fated *Bournemouth* of 1884 or the Clyde veteran *Venus* of 1852, had twin funnels, one fore and one aft of the paddles, but this was less common.

Many of these early steamers were privately owned, but as the fashion for seaside holidays and steamer trips grew, many of the smaller operators were forced out of business by the formation of newer, larger companies. These companies frequently came into direct competition for the custom available at the various resorts, and in order to attract passengers were forced to build larger and better steamers. The chief defect of the flush-decked paddler was the lack of sheltered accommodation. In poor weather passengers were faced with a choice between braving the wet and cold on the open main deck, or crowding below into the lower deck saloons from which they could see nothing of the scenery. Some companies attempted to overcome the problem by rigging deck awnings, but these were a poor substitute for the logical solution – namely the fitting of deck saloons.

The earliest of these took the form of isolated deck-houses on the main deck fore and aft, but by the mid 1870s it became common practice for saloons to be built immediately adjoining the forward or after end of the engine house amidships, and covered by an extension of the bridge deck, to form a small promenade deck which passengers paid a small supplement to use. All of these early deck saloons were narrow

affairs with alleyways on either side, giving access to the engine space. The Weymouth steamers *Empress* (1879) and *Victoria* (1884) were the last survivors of this breed. Both were fitted with small, short saloons on their after decks, and originally had isolated deck houses aft which were removed later in their careers. The two little ships lasted for many years and were finally broken up in 1955 and 1953 respectively. The Clyde boasted a large number of examples – all bigger, faster, and generally more magnificent than the little Weymouth ships – of which Gilles and Campbell's *Adela* of 1877, with her short saloons fore and aft, may be taken as typical.

Once deck saloons had become established as the norm, they developed steadily in size. Remaining narrow all the while, they got longer and longer, so that by the 1880s it was common for the steamers to have a saloon extending the whole length of the after deck (except for a rope-handling deck on the stern), and either a short fore saloon or a completely open foredeck. One such was Captain Robert Campbell's famous *Waverley* of 1885 which left the Clyde to become the first vessel of the P & A Campbell 'White Funnel Fleet' in the Bristol Channel. On the south coast the design became practically universal, and with only small modifications lasted right the way through until the final disappearance of the paddle steamers from the area, when the *Princess Elizabeth* was withdrawn from her service on the Weymouth station after the season of 1966.

During the 1870s other variations appeared. Several vessels, like Robert Campbell's *Benmore* of 1876 and the nomadic *Brodick Castle* of 1878, were not fitted with deck saloons but had their upper deck aft raised to bulwark level, so that there was room for a large saloon beneath, and a second saloon or bar on a lower deck level. A few ships, such as the Belfast and County Down Railway's *Slieve Donard* (later Campbell's *Albion*) had their foredecks treated in a similar manner, but were fitted with conventional deck saloons aft; yet others, like Cosens' *Monarch* of 1888 and Campbell's *Scotia* of 1880, had short raised fo'c'sles.

The next major development took place during the 1890s, when various owners decided to extend the promenade decks on top of the deck saloons right forward to bow and aft to the stern. In some cases, such as the famous Thames vessels *Koh-i-Noor* and *Royal Sovereign* (built for the Victoria Steamboat Association's services to Southend, Clacton and Margate, etc) the promenade deck was supported on stanchions so that the foredeck beneath was still open to the attacks of heavy seas, but more commonly, as in the case of Campbell's Bristol Channel steamers *Britannia* and *Cambria* or the Southampton ship *Balmoral*, the sides of the hull were plated up to promenade level. This design became fairly standard amongst the larger pleasure steamers built before the First War, and many were exceedingly beautiful. The long, uncluttered promenade deck, broken only by the paddle boxes, funnels and navigation bridge, served to emphasise the lovely sheer of these vessels, which in an era of hot competition and racing were often capable of high speeds.

The final development in pre-1914 steamer design is best illustrated by looking at the famous and incomparable *La Marguerite* of 1894. This vast steamer, the biggest excursion paddler ever built, measured 350 ft × 40 ft × 13 ft 6 in with a tonnage of 1,554 and was built to inaugurate a daily service between Tilbury Pier and Boulogne, returning the same day. Her introduction made it possible for the first time to sail to France and back in a day from London, and her luxurious accommodation made her a great favourite with the travelling public. In addition to having a full-length promenade deck, she was fitted with an upper deck which ran from the stern to just abaft the foremast and extended to the full width of the vessel. Beneath this deck was more accommodation, and the huge steamer was able to boast such sophistications as a hairdressing saloon and a post office. Although no other excursion steamer ever approached *La Marguerite* in magnificence, many developed along similar lines and sported deck houses and upper decks on top of their full-length promenade decks.

Just as the outward design of the steamers evolved, so did their engines. Many early ships were fitted with simple, single-expansion engines, but as boilers improved and steam pressures rose, compound engines became more common. Vertical engines of the 'steeple' and oscillating types were popular in the flush decked vessels, but, as steamers became larger and more sophisticated, diagonal engines became popular. The simple, single-cylinder, diagonal engines were somewhat unsatisfactory on account of the fore and aft surging motion they caused on board the steamer, their low efficiency, and their unfortunate tendency to stick on dead centre if the engine came to rest with the piston at the end of its stroke. The more satisfactory successors to this type of engine were the compound diagonal and triple expansion types which became the most popular power sources in the vessels of the 1880s and 90s, continuing to be fitted to paddlers right up until the last example of the sea going excursion paddler was launched in 1947.

The variety of trips available to the Victorian or Edwardian holidaymaker was enormous. In the early days, trips were organised more or less on whim, or as the demand arose. There are records of the town criers in several south-coast ports announcing hurriedly organised voyages to view landslides, dead whales, shipwrecks, launching ceremonies of major warships, or even garden parties and fêtes! It should be remembered that many of the first ships were primarily engaged in ferry or towage duties, and the provision of excursions meant that they had to be removed from their regular duties. However, as the true pleasure steamer evolved, summer excursions became increasingly regular, and more and more imaginative. By the 1840s it was possible to sail occasionally from the south-coast ports to Cherbourg or the Channel Islands (such excursions taking two or three days), as well as on a host of shorter, regular routes. On the Clyde and Thames the variety was even greater than elsewhere, for excursions could be taken on vessels which maintained regular sailings on fixed routes between numerous waterside communities. Indeed, many of our most famous pleasure steamers also maintained important utilitarian transport links in the Bristol Channel, Clyde, Thames, Western Isles and elsewhere.

Before the First War it would have been possible, with careful planning and a little luck, for a determined traveller to sail round most of the British coast in excursion paddle steamers. The sailing bills at large resorts proclaimed a staggering choice of trips, and steamer companies offered season tickets and other concessionary fares to regular passengers in order to win trade from their rivals. Racing between rival steamers was commonplace, although, following a number of collisions and boiler explosions, it was officially frowned upon. Several of the 'crack' long-distance steamers were capable of speeds in excess of 18 knots. Around the turn of the century a would-be passenger at Bournemouth could choose a quiet run to Swanage or Lulworth Cove, a long day to Torquay, Brighton, Alderney or even Cherbourg, or compromise with a half-day sailing to the Isle of Wight resorts or a wide variety of other destinations.

As previously mentioned, most large resorts had piers or landing stages, but it should not be supposed that pleasure steamers failed to visit less well-endowed places. Landing passengers by small boat was commonplace at spots such as Lynmouth and Clovelly in the Bristol Channel, at Staffa in the Western Isles and at a number of other places. On the south coast between Plymouth and Swanage an even more daring procedure was developed for landing passengers on the open beaches at resorts such as Budleigh Salterton, Seaton, Sidmouth and West Bay. The coasting steamers were fitted with hingeing landing stages, one end of which was attached to the vessel's port bow, and the other end hoisted upwards when at sea by a tackle attached to the fore deck. As the vessel approached the beach, she would drop two kedge anchors, and then gently run her especially strengthened forefoot onto the shingle. Held in position by her engines and anchors, the vessel would then land her passengers by way of a small door in the forward bulwarks and the springy landing stage, which had been lowered onto the beach. The operation completed, the vessel would hoist the stage, haul off on the kedges and proceed to the next beach! This risky performance often resulted in passengers being stranded for the night if a swell developed during the day and prevented the steamer from landing on the return journey! Surprisingly, however, only one steamer engaged in the coasting trade – the *Duchess of Devonshire* – was wrecked, when her kedge anchor cable broke and she broached to on Sidmouth beach in 1934.

It is amazing that there were not more casualties amongst excursion steamers generally, for in the days before radar or radio, hundreds of vessels were running from Easter until October in all kinds of weather. Schedules were maintained whenever possible, and steamers put to sea in extremely bad conditions, whilst those engaged in the long-distance trade were often caught out by gales at the far end of their runs, and had little option but to battle homewards. Exciting days! Needless to say, accidents did occur, and foggy weather was, perhaps, the greatest cause. Excursion steamers by their nature plied their trade as close as possible to the picturesque and dangerous coast and were therefore particularly vulnerable if caught in a sudden fog. On 27 August 1886 the *Bournemouth* was homeward bound from Torquay to Bournemouth when she was caught in a fog in Lyme Bay. Her captain miscalculated his distance run and altered course too soon, with the result that his two-year-old steamer became a total loss on the west side of Portland Bill. Fortunately, however, most steamer captains were highly skilled, careful men, and incidents of this type were few.

Many steamers carried small bands on board to entertain the passengers and contemporary newspapers were full of accounts of bands 'discoursing sweet music' to which the passengers, or at least those who were 'votaries of Terpsichore', would on occasions dance or sing. Dining saloons provided meals and snacks at all times of the day at a quality and price which in comparison to today's fare seem like fantasy! One steamer company's tariff dated 1909, lists a choice of three cooked breakfasts, ten luncheons (including lobster), six high teas, plus a choice of three champagnes and numerous hocks, burgundies, clarets, liqueurs and ales!

Finally, it should be said that paddle steamers were ideal vessels for the excursion trade. Their broad decks and sea-kindly qualities made them perfect for the carriage of large numbers of passengers in relative comfort, and their manoeuvrability and responsiveness to engine orders made them well-suited to a coastal trade in which much time was spent berthing alongside piers or cruising in busy rivers or sea-lanes. After the 1914–18 war, in which many of the finest ships were lost, it is true that a gradual decline set in, but for all that it is no coincidence that the excursion paddle steamer survived in considerable numbers until the 1960s. Even today we have one fine example in the form of the Waverley Steam Navigation Company's magnificent Clyde steamer *Waverley* – a worthy successor to her ancestors of the Victorian and Edwardian periods.

96 Looking rather the worse for wear, the *Marquis of Bute* is pictured on the Clyde, *c.*1900, painted in the Glasgow & South Western Railway's attractive livery of grey hull, white upperworks and a red, black-topped funnel. Built in 1868 for the Rothesay service operated by her owner and skipper, Sandy McLean, she was one of the fastest and most popular Clyde steamers of her day. She originally conformed to the classic, Clyde flush-decked design, but a small deck saloon and a raised bridge were added later in her life.

97 Cosens & Company's *Victoria* and *Empress* landing passengers at Lulworth Cove, Dorset, in 1906. *Victoria* (nearest the camera) has arrived first on an afternoon cruise from Weymouth and landed her passengers over the bows by way of a wheeled landing stage pulled out from the shore. *Empress* has arrived a few minutes later and has gone alongside her to unload her passengers over her sister's decks. When they were broken up during the 1950s these little vessels were the last examples of flush-decked steamers with small deck saloons. The rusting remains of the landing stages can be seen to this day on the beach in the Cove

98 RIGHT The engine room of the *Empress*. This compact set of 52 N.H.P. oscillating engines were built in 1879 by John Penn of Greenwich and had two cylinders with a diameter of 30 in and a stroke of 33 in. When the ship ran her trials on the Thames on 15 May 1879 she achieved a mean speed of 13.2 knots over the measured mile on a boiler pressure of only 29 lbs per square inch. The engines were extremely economical and it was said in Weymouth that the *Empress* 'would go round the Shambles lightship on a shovel of coal'! They were the last operational set of oscillating engines in Britain, and are now preserved in the Southampton Maritime Museum

99 BELOW The Devon Dock, Pier and Steamship Company's *Duke of Devonshire* of 1896 backing away from the open beach at West Bay, Bridport, after landing passengers by means of her hingeing landing stage, the construction of which can be seen clearly in this fine view. These clumsy but ingenious contraptions must have suffered frequent damage as the coasting steamers pitched their way across the swell for which Lyme Bay is notorious

100 LEFT An alternative means of disembarkation: passengers landing by small boat from the *Brighton Queen* off Newhaven in 1900

101 RIGHT En route for Swanage and Bournemouth, Cosens & Company's *Monarch* of 1888 is seen here backing away from Weymouth pier. Her raised fo'c'sle, thin funnels and narrow deck saloon gave her a rather antiquated appearance, but she was a fine seaboat and up to the First War was closely associated with the day trips from Bournemouth to Alderney. She also ran to Cherbourg and on long coastal trips, and was not broken up until 1950

102 BELOW The classic profile of the MacBrayne steamer *Grenadier* is emphasised in this view of her landing passengers by boat at the Island of Iona, sometime before 1902. This lovely ship spent most of her life running summer excursions from Oban to Staffa and Iona, and operating a winter service to Ardishaig, her economical but unconventional compound oscillating engines making her particularly suitable for all-year-round use. Her working life came to a tragic end when she caught fire at Oban pier late one night in September 1927. Her master and several of her crew were killed in the blaze and the old steamer was so badly damaged that she was broken up at Ardrossan in the following year

103 BELOW The *Bournemouth* was wrecked on the west side of Portland Bill in a thick fog at 6.50 p.m. on 27 August 1886. Although all her passengers were taken off safely in small boats, and much of her gear was saved, the ship broke her back just forward of the engine space and became a total loss. One of the nameboards from her bows was discovered a few years ago in a house on the Isle of Portland, and is now displayed in the Weymouth Museum

104 LEFT This unusual view shows work in progress at J. & G. Thompson's Clyde shipyard on the assembly of one of the paddle wheels for the Belfast & County Down Railway's steamer *Slieve Bearnagh* during 1894. The paddle floats had not yet been fitted to the wheel, but were clearly intended to be of the feathering type

105 BELOW The Caledonian Steam Packet Company's *Galatea* of 1889 was a handsome ship, but was fitted with engines that were too powerful for her hull, with the consequence that she could never be driven as hard as her looks might have suggested. She was sold to owners in Genoa in 1906, and scrapped in 1913.

106 LEFT Swinging astern from the quay at Gorleston is the 18 knot *Southend Belle*, one of the seven famous 'Belle Steamers' built by Denny of Dumbarton between 1890 and 1900 for service in the Thames estuary and along the Norfolk, Essex and Kent coasts. From their base at Fresh Wharf near London Bridge, these fast ships offered day trips as far as Yarmouth in the north and Ramsgate to the south. *Southend Belle* spent much of her time on the service to Ramsgate via Margate, but was also used on the longer Yarmouth route which took two days for the round trip. Two steamers were employed, leaving on alternate days from each end and crossing at Walton, where day trippers could change ships and return to their starting point the same day, or catch a connecting steamer to Ipswich

107 ABOVE This famous but irresistible photograph of Ilfracombe pier was taken in 1895 and illustrates the characteristics of several generations of local pleasure steamers. They are, from left to right: Campbell's *Ravenswood* of 1891; Edwards, Robertsons & Company's *Lorna Doone* of 1891; three more Campbell ships, the *Bonnie Doon* of 1876 (immortalised as the 'Bonnie Breakdoon' due to her unreliability during her early days on the Clyde!), the *Cambria* of 1895 and the *Westward Ho!* of 1894; the Cardiff tug *Earl of Dunraven* of 1888, which ran summer excursions from Cardiff and Weston to Ilfracombe and Watchet; and the veteran *Alexandra*, originally built in 1854 as the Weymouth & Channel Islands S.P. Company's *Aquila* for the service to Jersey and Guernsey

108 Captain N. E. 'Satan' Hucker (seated centre) and the crew of Edwards, Robertsons & Company's Bristol Channel steamer *Lorna Doone*, at Ilfracombe pier, 10 August 1894

109 A shaft of sunlight from the deck above illuminates the magnificent, compound diagonal machinery of the Campbell flyer *Cambria*. These powerful engines, built by Messrs. Hutson & Company of Glasgow in 1895, developed 304 N.H.P. and were capable of driving the ship at over 21 knots, making her one of the fastest excursion paddle steamers ever to sail in British waters

110 ABOVE, RIGHT Victorian furnishing at its most magnificent: this view of the spacious main saloon of the Caledonian Steam Packet Company's *Duchess of Rothesay* of 1895, gives a splendid impression of the amount of detailed work which went in to the interior of a Victorian pleasure steamer. The photograph was taken looking forward towards the flight of steps which led up to the promenade deck above. Note the inevitable aspidistras which flank the entrance!

111 One of the lower saloons in another of the same company's ships, the *Duchess of Fife*, built in 1903 by the Fairfield Shipbuilding & Engineering Company of Govan. The painted panels, gleaming oil lamps and buttoned velvet upholstery combined to give a cosy atmosphere to this saloon, which was heated by an ornate cast-iron stove, just visible on the left of the picture

112 Crowds of passengers on Rothesay pier watch the arrival of the most famous and prestigious Clyde steamer of all time, the MacBrayne flagship *Columba*. The ship was built in 1878 of steel – a considerable innovation at the time – and was magnificently finished internally and externally. She spent her whole life on the Glasgow to Ardishaig mail service, for which she was designed, and gained the patronage of the nobility and gentry who travelled in her to their hunting lodges and houses in the Western Isles, as well as that of thousands of Glasgow day-trippers. *Columba* carved a unique place for herself in the affections of the Scottish public and was sorely missed when, after 58 years on the Royal Route, she was finally broken up in 1936

113 LEFT In this photograph, taken on 15 July 1902, the painters at John Brown's Clydebank shipyard are seen putting the finishing touches to the paintwork of the Brighton, Worthing & South Coast Steamboat Company's magnificent *Brighton Queen*, shortly before she sailed on her delivery voyage to Newhaven. With her speed of 20 knots, she was designed to run long-distance trips from Brighton, and at the time of her delivery outclassed all other steamers on the South Coast. Her original design incorporated a number of unusual features, all of which are illustrated by this photograph. Firstly, her main deck saloons were narrow and flanked by alleyways which, although covered by the full width promenade deck, were open to the wind and spray; secondly she had two bridges. The after one between the paddle boxes bore the engine room telegraphs and was connected by a catwalk to the second one, forward of the funnel, where the wheelhouse was located. The reason for these curious features is unclear, but after the ship was taken over by P & A Campbell in 1901 the alleyways were plated in, and the after bridge was converted into a 'reserve' passenger deck. *Brighton Queen* was the most beautiful and best-loved of all Sussex steamers, but had a tragically short life. On the night of 5 October 1915, whilst minesweeping off the Belgian coast, she struck a mine and foundered

114 The legendary *La Marguerite* at Boulogne, *c*.1898. This enormous paddler was built on the Clyde by Fairfields in 1894 to inaugurate the first regular day-return service from London to Boulogne, but her owners, the Victoria Steamboat Association, were soon in financial trouble and the ship's management passed to New Palace Steamers Limited, in whose plain yellow funnel colours she appears in this photograph. Her massive engines were veritable coal eaters and the ship proved a financial embarrassment to her owners, who eventually sold her to the Liverpool & North Wales S.S. Company in 1904. With the exception of the war years, she spent the rest of her life running excursions from the Mersey to Llandudno and the Menai Straits and was finally scrapped in 1925

115 LEFT This picture, taken at John Brown's shipyard at Clydebank, shows the spacious promenade deck of the Barry Railway Company's *Gwalia*, shortly before she ran her trials. She and her sister ship *Devonia* operated excursions from Cardiff and Barry on the Bristol Channel, where their fine accommodation and high speed made them worthy competitors to the larger P & A Campbell 'White Funnel Fleet'. In 1910 the *Gwalia* was sold to the Furness Railway, who renamed her *Lady Moyra* and used her on their service from Fleetwood to Barrow. A year later the rest of the Barry Railway fleet — *Barry*, *Devonia* and *Westonia* — passed into Campbell's hands, to be joined in 1922 by the *Lady Moyra* which, having finally passed into the ownership of her old competitors, became the second *Brighton Queen*

116 LEFT The beautifully decorated, streamlined paddle-boxes of the *Gwalia* bore her owner's rampant lion crest — a device which was also etched into the glass of most of the deck saloon windows

117 The foredeck of the Furness Railway's *Lady Evelyn*, en route from Fleetwood to Barrow on 28 July 1909. A train connected with the steamer at Barrow and enabled Blackpool holidaymakers to enjoy a day in the Lake District, where the company's lake steamers offered excursions on Lake Windermere. This photograph was taken on a breezy day, with the steamer lifting her bows to the choppy waters of Morecambe Bay. Many of the passengers seem more intent on keeping warm or preventing their hats from blowing overboard than on listening to the ship's three-piece band, which includes a harp!

127

118 LEFT Captain James on the bridge of the *Albion* at Eastbourne pier in 1914, shortly before the steamer left on her regular 5 p.m. sailing to Brighton. *Albion* was built as the *Slieve Donard* for the Belfast and County Down Railway in 1893, and was purchased by Campbells in 1899. She still holds the record for the fastest trip between Brighton and Eastbourne, in a time of 66 minutes

119 RIGHT Pictured on the stocks shortly before her launch from John Brown's Clydebank yard in March 1902 is the Glasgow & South Western Railway's *Mars*. A pretty, single-funnelled steamer with a full length promenade deck, she survived the First War only to be run down and sunk by a destroyer whilst minesweeping off Harwich, after the armistice, on 18 November 1918

120 BELOW All excursion sailings were advertised to operate subject to 'weather and circumstances permitting'. This impressive view of the *Cambria* of 1896 plunging along off Ilfracombe in the teeth of a gale gives some idea of the bad conditions in which many steamers continued to put to sea, and dispels any notion that these 'summer butterflies' were poor seaboats. A group of stout-hearted passengers can be seen huddled in the lee of the funnel seeking some degree of protection from the spray which is sheeting over the foredeck

121 *Golden Eagle*, the last Thames steamer to be built before the First World War, is seen here fitting out at John Brown's yard in 1909. Her owners, the General Steam Navigation Company, had taken delivery of a triple-screw turbine steamer, the *Kingfisher*, in time for the 1906 season, but the innovation was not a success and the company reverted to paddle propulsion for the *Golden Eagle*. She was fitted with the first set of triple-expansion engines in the fleet and was normally employed on the London Bridge to Margate and Ramsgate service. Note the wheel on the fo'c'sle for the bow rudder – a necessity in ships which proceeded up the final few miles of the Thames stern first, to avoid the difficulties of turning in the river off Fresh Wharf

122 The end of the era. This photograph was taken at Bournemouth pier on 4 August 1914, the day on which England declared war on Germany. Unlike many of her contemporaries this steamer, the ever popular *Bournemouth Queen*, survived the war, but it is sobering to ponder upon how few of the male excursionists lived to walk the decks of a pleasure steamer again

Bibliography

BEAVER, P.   *The Big Ship*, Hugh Evelyn, 1969 (A pictorial history of the 'Great Eastern')

BODY, G.   *British Paddle Steamers*, David & Charles, 1971

BURTT, F.   *Cross Channel and Coastal Paddle Steamers*, R. Tilling, 1934
   Steamers of the Thames and Medway, R. Tilling, 1949

BUSK, H.   *The Navies of the World*, 1859, Reprinted by the Richmond Publishing Company, 1971

CLOWES, SIR W.L.   *The Royal Navy, A History*, (7 vols), Sampson Lowe & Marsden, 1903

COLLEDGE, J.J.   *Ships of the Royal Navy*, (2 vols), David & Charles, 1969

COTON, R.H.   *A Decline of the Paddle Steamer*, Paddle Steamer Preservation Society, 1971

D'ORLEY, A.   *The Humber Ferries*, Nidd Valley Narrow Gauge Railway Ltd., 1968

DUCKWORTH, C.L.D. &   *Railway & Other Steamers*, (2nd Ed.) T. Stephenson & Sons Ltd., 1968
LANGMUIR, G.E.   *West Coast Steamers*, (2nd Ed.) T. Stephenson & Sons Ltd., 1956
      Clyde & Other Coastal Steamers, Brown, Son & Ferguson, 1939
      Clyde River & Other Steamers, (2nd Ed.) Brown, Son & Ferguson, 1946
      West Highland Steamers, (2nd Ed.) Richard Tilling, 1950

DUGAN, J.   *The Great Iron Ship*, Hamish Hamilton, 1953

FARR, G.   *West Country Passenger Steamers*, (2nd Ed.) T. Stephenson & Sons Ltd., 1967

GAVIN, C.M.   *Royal Yachts*, Rich & Gowan, 1932

GODFREY, A.   *Pleasure Steamers of Old Yorkshire*, A. Godfrey

GRIGSBY, J.E.   *Annals of our Royal Yachts*, Adlard Coles, 1953

GRIMSHAW, G.   *British Pleasure Steamers 1920–39*, Richard Tilling, 1945

GUTHRIE, J.   *Bizarre Ships of the Nineteenth Century*, Hutchinson, 1970

HAMBLETON, F.C.   *Famous Paddle Steamers*, Percival Marshall & Company, 1948

HENRY, F.   *Ships of the Isle of Man Steam Packet Company Ltd.*, (4th Ed.) Brown, Son & Ferguson, 1977

LINGWOOD, J.E.   *By Royal Charter – The Steam Conquistadores – A History of the Pacific Steam Navigation Company*, P.S.N.C. 1977

LUCKING, J.   *The Great Western at Weymouth*, David & Charles, 1971

MCGOWAN, A.P.   *Royal Yachts*, National Maritime Museum, 1977

MCMURRAY, H.C.   *Old Order, New Thing*, National Maritime Museum, 1972 (P.S. Reliant and the Manchester Ship Canal Tugs)

MCNEILL, D.B.   *Irish Passenger Steamship Services*, (2 vols.) David & Charles, 1971

O'BRIEN, F.T.   *Early Solent Steamers*, David & Charles, 1973

O'CONNOR, G.W.   *The First Hundred Years*, Red Funnel Steamers, 1961

PATERSON, A.J.S.   *The Victorian Summer of the Clyde Steamers*, David & Charles, 1972
   The Golden Years of the Clyde Steamers, David & Charles, 1969

SPRATT, P.   *Transatlantic Paddle Steamers*, (2nd Ed.) Brown, Son & Ferguson, 1967

THORNLEY, F.C.   *Steamers of North Wales*, (2nd Ed.) T. Stephenson & Sons, 1962

THORNTON, E.C.B.   *South Coast Pleasure Steamers*, T. Stephenson & Son, 1960
   Thames Coast Pleasure Steamers, T. Stephenson & Sons, 1972

THURSTON, G.   *The Great Thames Disaster*, George, Allen & Unwin, 1965 (The Story of the 'Princess Alice' Disaster)

MAGAZINES
Sea Breezes, Ships Monthly, Ship Ahoy (Journal of the South Wales Branch of the World Ship Society) and *Paddle Wheels* (Journal of the Paddle Steamer Preservation Society)

Index

Numerals in *italics* refer to the figure numbers

135

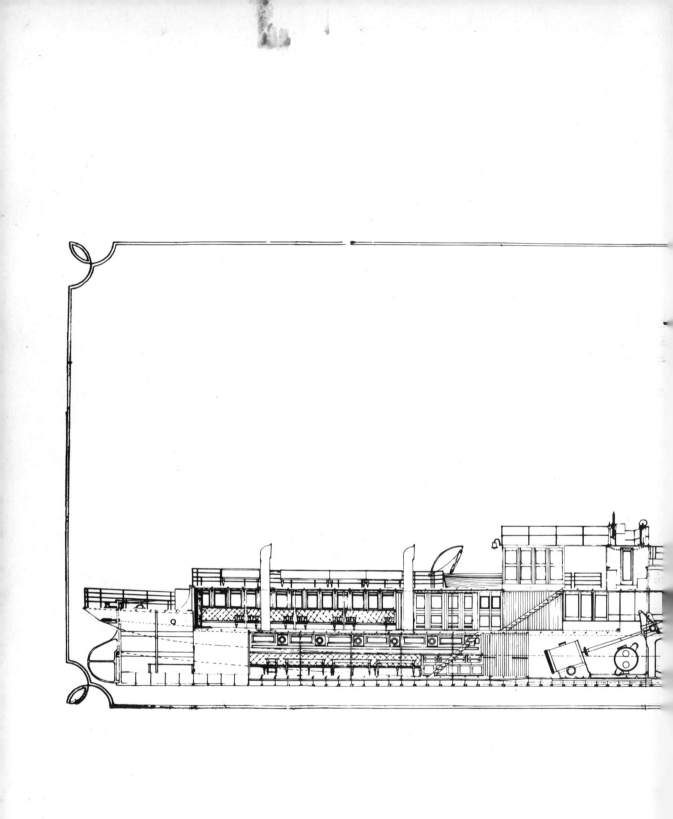